Battle of the Reichswald

Peter Elstob

Battle of the Reichswald

Editor-in-Chief: Barrie Pitt
Art Director: Peter Dunbar
Military Consultant: Sir Basil Liddell Hart
Picture Editor: Bobby Hunt
Editor: David Mason
Design: Sarah Kingham
Special Drawings: John Batchelor
Cartographer: Richard Natkiel
Cover: Denis Piper
Photographic Research: Nan Shuttleworth

ISBN 0-345-27901-8

Manufactured in the United States of America

First Edition: December 1970
Second Printing: November 1978

Contents

$1.50

Operation Veritable

Introduction by Lieutenant-General Sir Brian Horrocks, Commander XXX Corps

On the 8th February 1944 I climbed into my command post, which consisted of a small platform half way up a tree, from where I could see in front of me a peaceful looking valley with small farms dotted here and there. On the far side lay the sinister Reichswald Forest. Over this valley XXX Corps were about to attack.

In a way it was a thrilling moment. We had come a long way and here at last lay Germany itself. But I always hated the last few minutes before zero hour and kept going over in my mind all the detailed plans, wondering whether everything possible had been done to give the leading troops a fair fighting chance. I could just imagine the drawn look on the men's faces. Being British, they were of course making jokes. I once saw four men in an armoured carrier cross the start line for an attack wearing their black top hats which all Germans keep for funerals. This showed a macabre sense of humour but it was typical. But however much the troops may joke, they are under no illusions about what lies before them.

A corps is the highest formation which actually fights the battle; the echelons above us – army group, army etc, – are chiefly concerned with strategical problems. Battles cannot be run like board meetings and though a wise commander will always listen carefully to the advice of his experts ultimately the plan is his and his alone. Few people realise what a heavy responsibility rests on a corps commander's shoulders and what appalling decisions he is called to make. We formed part of the First Canadian Army and a few days earlier General Crerar the army commander had asked me whether I wanted the German town of Cleve 'taking out': by that he meant obliterated by Bomber Command. Cleve was an old historical German Rhineland city. Anne of Cleves, Henry VIII's fourth wife, came from there; no doubt its inhabitants included many civilians, probably women and children among them. Unfortunately the key to the preliminary stages of this battle depended on a race between the 15th Scottish Division and the German reserves for the Nutterden feature which dominated the main corridor between Cleve and the Reichswald through which we hoped to break out into the German plains beyond, and there was no doubt that the German reserves would have to come through Cleve. The lives of one's own men must come first, so I said 'yes', but I did not enjoy seeing those heavy bombers flying overhead on their deadly mission. And this decision caused me many a nightmare for years after the war was over; perhaps I have too much imagination ever to have risen to great heights in the military hierachy and fortunately for the British I never did. All battles are terrible, but luckily for my peace of mind I did not then realise that this was only the start of the worst battle I ever experienced which was to last for approximately one month during which some part of my corps would be attacking every day and every night.

What was so maddening was that the whole thing could have been so easy if only the frost had continued.

Perhaps the gods in their wisdom decided that the odds were too much in our favour, because the whole elaborate plan was nullified by the one thing over which we had no control, namely the weather. I seem to remember that it rained almost every day, added to which the Germans breached the banks of the Rhine, so instead of the lovely hard frozen 'going', we were faced by oceans of mud and water and within ten minutes of the start every tank – in fact every vehicle – was bogged down and the water started to spread across our one road to Nijmegen-Cleve.

I have no intention of following the course of the battle in detail because this has been accurately, clearly and fairly described by Peter Elstob. I am particularly glad that he has dealt in some detail with the events leading up to the battle, particularly with the administration arrangements which are so often overlooked by historians.

The Germans knew that a large scale offensive was about to be launched by the Allies but it was vital to prevent their finding out where it would come. This meant that the concentration of some 170,000 troops plus mountains of equipment and stores of all kinds had to be moved into the woods south of Nijmegen without the Germans knowing anything about it, and the fact that this succeeded so well was the result of some of the most brilliant staff work I ever came in contact with during the war. I can say this because it was really nothing to do with me. XXX Corps staff had been together before Alamein and in the course of their long journeying through the desert, along the north coast of Africa,

Sicily, Italy, Normandy, France, Belgium and Holland the weaker brethren had fallen by the wayside, so in taking over this corps in Normandy I inherited probably the best staff in any army which took part in the last war. Under my brilliant Chief of Staff (BGS) Brigadier C P Jones who ended his career on the Army Council, they were a tough highly intelligent group of young staff officers who could take in their stride any of the crises which constantly occur in war, which was just as well, because when the thaw suddenly set in and the bottom literally dropped out of several vital roads, it resulted in a crisis of no small magnitude. Yet the attack went in on time and for the first twenty-four hours the Germans had no idea at all as to the magnitude of the blow which had hit them.

After the initial attacks this was a battle in which generalship played no part at all: it developed into a slogging match in the mud between the regimental officers, NCOs and men: in fact it became a CO's battle. Each day I used to leave my HQ in a jeep at approximately 8 am and go round 'smelling the battlefield', not I am afraid with any recipe for victory in my pocket but to do my best to lift morale by visiting HQs and units which I knew were having a bad time. I used to listen sympathetically to their tales of woe. I would then try and slip some item of good news quite casually into the conversation and one could almost feel the atmosphere lightening. I hoped that when I left, the poor exhausted adjutant or brigade major, who probably hadn't slept for forty-eight hours, would say 'Well, things don't seem so bad after all'.

May I finish with a tribute to the young soldiers, many of them almost straight from Britain who fought night and day in the freezing rain and the mud against some of the best German troops from the parachute and panzer divisions – and beat them.

'The best laid plans...'

'Operations actually developed rather differently and less rapidly due to interference by the enemy.' Stacey, *The Victory Campaign.*

In war life seldom imitates art but the Battle of the Reichswald might well have been devised as a tactical problem in a War Game. The advantages and disadvantages, the checks and balances, were most carefully distributed and the defender, though heavily outmanned and outgunned, was greatly favoured by the geography and enjoyed a wide choice of moves. The problems posed were not the usual ones for which standard answers could be found and the attacker's overwhelming material superiority was partly offset by the limitations imposed upon him.

In the first place the scene of battle was rigidly circumscribed by flooded rivers. secondly, a major natural obstacle lay just in front of the start line – a thick forest five miles wide and eight miles deep. thirdly, only two main roads ran in the direction of the attack. fourthly, the defence was extremely varied, consisting of infantry trenches, mortar and machine gun positions, mobile guns, anti-tank ditches and barbed wire all arranged in three successive lines and, finally, the main objectives, two ring-fortified towns beyond the forest, were further protected by high ground occupied by forces who completely dominated the only possible approach roads.

A sudden thaw a week before the offensive completely upset the attackers' long-thought-out plan by limiting the employment of tanks and other vehicles to the roads, and these – apart from main ones – were largely unsurfaced forest tracks only wide enough for a single line of vehicles. The trees were too closely planted for tanks, half-tracks or even jeeps to penetrate. Roads ran in check pattern through and across the forest which meant that the defenders could

hit cross roads with fire from two or three directions. The cover was ideal for snipers.

From all this it will be readily realised that the ground greatly favoured the defence and in a War Game such an advantage would be compensated and this was so in the real battle. The attacker had complete air superiority which enabled him to discover the main defence positions, to keep an accurate check on changes in dispositions, re-inforcements, the availability of bridges, the location of bottle-necks and the extent of the flooding. He was also able to deny aerial reconnaissance to his adversary and thus conceal the extent of his own build-up. Before the battle began his massed artillery and air force were able to deal out paralysing blows on every observed position and on the main objectives.

On the other hand, almost as if the problem setter had wanted to make sure that this great material superiority did not swing the balance too much the other way, the defender had been granted time to construct a defence in depth which would allow him to choose where to fight and to accumulate and deploy a mobile reserve. The scales thus being more or less evenly balanced a few imponderables were thrown in: the weather could completely alter the tactical situation at any time, for a hard frost would enable a wide-front advance while prolonged rain would increase the flooded area and the depth of the mud. Lastly the defender had a once-only weapon – 160 million cubic metres of water held by dams behind his left flank. By releasing this suddenly he could wipe out a second attacking force attempting to encircle his rear, by keeping the sluice gates open he could create and maintain a vast flooded area which would last for some two weeks and protect his left flank. The defenders' right flank was protected by flood extending all the way to a mighty river which turned and ran behind right across the

The Siegfried Line scars the countryside

entire front. The seizing of crossings over this river and the establishing of bridgeheads were the objectives of the offensive in which breaking through the fortified forest was the opening move.

These objectives gave the battle strategic as well as tactical importance, for the attackers had based the final campaign of the war on this breakthrough and subsequent exploitation and for their part the defenders well realised that the small wooded area across a strip of land between two rivers was the plug blocking an entry which led into the heart of their country.

All the circumstances, then, were carefully balanced at the beginning of the Battle of the Reichswald but it was not a War Game but bitter, relentless battle and before the real problem was solved, ancient, beautiful towns would be completely destroyed and thousands of human beings – women and children as well as soldiers – would be killed or maimed. Intended to be all over in three or four days the assault slogged on for more than two weeks and no one who fought on either side in those terrible conditions will ever forget them. Many soldiers were drowned in the floods and in the mud – mud so deep that it swallowed not only men and guns but huge Churchill tanks. The conditions in and around the Reichswald Forest in February 1945, when British and Canadian soldiers struggled to turn the German Siegfried Line, were unique on the Western Front in the Second World War and parts of the front resembled that of Passchendaele.

On both sides the fighting was carried on with quite remarkable ferocity, tenacity and courage. Remarkable on the German side because so many of them must have known that the war was lost, because the odds against them were overwhelming, because they were without air cover and because most were practically without infantry training. On the Allies' side the attack came after

many postponements during which the Germans had been seen to be building a most formidable defence, many of the infantry regiments had had nine long months of war and belonged to divisions with the highest casualties in 21st Army Group. Finally when the order to attack came the sudden thaw which preceded it produced the worst conditions of the war for infantry and armour on the Western Front.

Although the attack finally prevailed the defence was so determined and so skilful it upset the attackers' time-table which in turn brought about major strategic changes. These could not, of course, prevent Germany's defeat; nothing could have by that time except possession of the atom bomb.

The long term result of the prolonged and bitter fighting at the extreme end of the Siegfried Line was probably to shorten the last phase of the war – or at least to enable the Western Allies to advance as far east as they did before Berlin fell to the Russians. The reason for this conclusion is that Hitler's emotional reaction to the penetration of the Siegfried Line was to forbid any retreat and to send all available reserves north in an attempt to stop the British and Canadians. This left the centre of the Siegfried Line gravely undermanned and the American forces, who had earlier suffered their heaviest casualties trying to break into Germany through the Aachen area suddenly found the going easier and were able to cross the Rhineland

Tank traps in the Siegfried Line

with surprisingly light casualties.

The battle with which this book is concerned, the Battle of the Reichswald Forest, the opening phase of Operation Veritable which began the campaign which was to end with Germany's unconditional surrender, was originally intended to start at the end of September, 1944, following the Arnhem Operation. It did not actually begin until over four months later and by then the chances of outflanking the comparatively light defences of the northern end of the Siegfried Line and slicing into the Ruhr with a fast, cheap offensive had been lost, for the Germans had been alerted to their weakness and had extended their defence line all the way to the Rhine

11

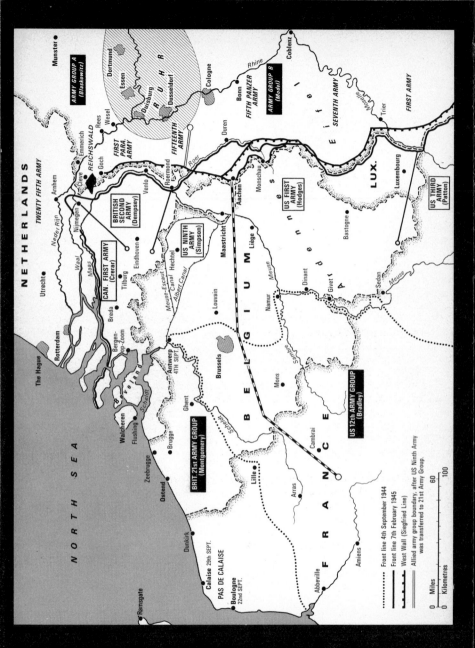

The situation before the battle, 7th February 1945

at Emmerich. They had also built a lesser Siegfried Line through the Reichswald Forest between the Meuse and the Rhine.

There were many reasons for the delay of which the most important were the failure to capture a bridgehead over the Neder Rijn at Arnhem, the supply difficulties caused by the delay in opening the port of Antwerp, the failure to realise early enough the importance of the German possession of the Roer dams and the failure of Allied Intelligence to assess the extent of the German recovery after the collapse of France and Belgium.

It was this astonishing recovery which enabled the Germans to turn and inflict a costly and strategically important defeat on the 1st US Army at Schmidt (see *The Battle of the Rhineland* by R W Thompson for a closely-reasoned argument for the importance of the Battle of Schmidt), to mount a successful counterattack against Montgomery's 2nd Army, which established a spoiling re-entry bridgehead across the Meuse and to put up so spirited a resistance in Holland that it took over three months to clear the area up to the Maas. Most important of all, it enabled them to launch the great Ardennes Offensive in December and thus most unexpectedly to regain the initiative. (At an Investiture for the 51st Highland Division on the day before this offensive was launched Montgomery told the assembled soldiers 'the German Army is on its knees and, having no petrol, will never again be able to mount an offensive.')

But to all these reasons for the Allies' loss of momentum in the last quarter of 1944 must be added the result of the rivalries and quarreling between some of the commanders at the highest level who, as soon as victory in Europe seemed to be certain, became almost as concerned with enhancing their own reputations as with the defeat of the common enemy.

Before attempting to follow the course of the Battle of the Reichswald we should know how the situation on the northern half of the Western Front at the beginning of February 1945 had come about. It is impossible to go back to the beginning for, particularly towards the end, every stage of a war is linked back to many others but, as far as the often postponed attack to outflank the Siegfried Line is concerned, the crucial question is why it took place in February 1945 instead of three or four months earlier. A good date to start to look for the answer is 1st September 1944 when Brussels fell and the great Allied advance from the Seine seemed about to sweep on in an irresistible flood.

It was on that day that General Eisenhower moved his headquarters to Europe and assumed the active role of Supreme Commander. General Montgomery, promoted to Field-Marshal to compensate for a *de facto* demotion, hoped that some sort of an arrangement could be worked out whereby he could continue to exercise 'full operational direction, control and co-ordination' of the ground troops – or at least of his own 21st Army Group and General Bradley's 12th Army Group – under General Eisenhower, who would be 'Supreme Commander', a job the full responsibilities of which were obviously not clear to Montgomery.

On 4th September the 11th Armoured Division captured Antwerp and its port installations intact. The importance of this could hardly be overestimated, for the logistic situation of the Western Allies' central and northern groups of armies was desperate and a deep water port was as necessary to continue the broad front advance as the men themselves, for it was no longer possible to keep them supplied and equipped from the Normandy beaches.

Hitler's insistence that the German garrisons in the channel ports, which had been bypassed by the Allies' advance, hang on to the 'last man and the last round' in order to deny these ports to allied shipping had forced an overstretching of the long lines of supply. By mid-September the explosive expansion of the front from the line of the Seine to one that ran from Antwerp to Metz had overtaxed not only the normal system but all the improvisations the ingenuity of the supply services had been able to contrive. Now it was not possible even for Montgomery's 'single powerful thrust' to be maintained without at least one deep water port.

The German Fifteenth Army, kept in the Pas de Calais area in expectation of a second invasion, had been pushed north-east up the coast by the

The formidable defences

Canadians. The drive to Antwerp had apparently trapped them with the North Sea to the west, the Allies to the east and the Scheldt to the north. More German forces occupied the island of Beveland on the other side of the Scheldt from which a single road ran east to the mainland. To the German High Command the situation of the Fifteenth Army on 4th September seemed desperate for they expected an immediate thrust from Antwerp to Breda, twenty-five miles north, which they knew they could not stop and which would cut off all their forces west of Antwerp and on Beveland. Nevertheless orders were sent to the army commander, General Schwabe, to withdraw a fairly strong force across the narrow western end of the Scheldt from Breskens to

Flushing and thence east through Bergen-op-Zoom and Breda. At the most it was hoped that some troops and equipment could be got away before the Allies sealed the escape route.

To the Germans' amazement the Allies made no move from Antwerp at all and in the next nineteen days 86,000 German soldiers and vast quantities of badly-needed equipment including 616 guns were ferried across the Scheldt to fight again. This was a double accomplishment for it also allowed the Germans to occupy both banks and thus deny the Scheldt to shipping and as Antwerp lies some sixty miles from the sea the great port could not be used.

It has often been asked why the tanks of the 11th Armoured Division

stopped in Antwerp. The straightforward answer is that our orders (the author commanded one of these tanks) were to seize and secure the port installations intact and that is precisely what was done. This throws the responsibility on a tactical level back on the corps commander, General Horrocks, and he has shouldered the blame handsomely.

In *A Full Life* he writes: 'At the time this (the capture of the docks) seemed the obvious objective, but I realise now that it was a serious mistake. My excuse is that my eyes were fixed entirely on the Rhine and everything else seemed of subsidiary importance. It never entered my head that the Scheldt would be mined and that we should not be able to use Antwerp port until the channel had been swept and the Germans cleared from the coastline on either side. Nor did I realise that the Germans would be able to evacuate a large number of the troops trapped in the coastal areas across the Scheldt.

'Napoleon would no doubt have realised these things but Horrocks didn't. His mind was fixed on the Rhine. I am not suggesting that with one armoured division I could have cleared both banks of the Scheldt estuary but I believe that I could have seriously impeded, if not stopped altogether, the evacuation of the German Fifteenth Army.'

The tactical shortsightedness could and should have been retrieved by strategic longsightedness and the opening up of the port of Antwerp have been given immediate, overriding priority. Instead it was shelved for the time being and priority given to a bold thrust aimed at the lower reaches of the Rhine some eighty miles northeast.

Not opening Antwerp was a major mistake and many attempts have been made to fix the blame but a cool, objective look at the facts leads to the conclusion that it was due to a number of things which, unfortunately for the Allies, all occurred at the same time:

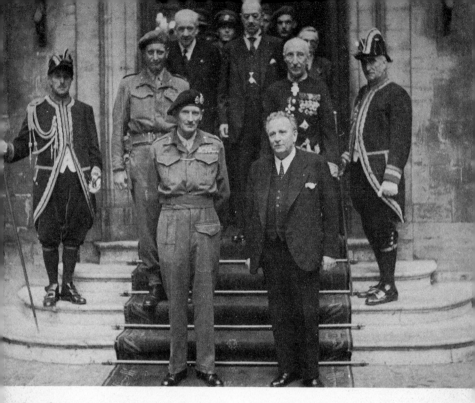

Above: The fall of Brussels.
Montgomery poses with the city
fathers. *Right:* Jubilant Brussels
citizens ride the British tanks

the changeover of command at the
top which took more time than it
should have done because it coincided
with Eisenhower being temporarily
out of action with an injured leg;
communications difficulties between
Eisenhower's HQ and his Army Group
commanders hundreds of miles away;
Montgomery's desire to retain control
of the ground forces coupled with his
conviction that the war could be
finished by one powerful blow from the
northern flank; Bradley's feeling that
his armies, particularly the Third
commanded by the rumbustious Patton, were being starved of supplies so
that the British could continue to
advance; the widely-held impression
that the Germans were completely
demoralised and could never regain
the initiative.

In other words it seemed to be the
time for a bold, imaginative stroke, a
lightning attack east which would
push the Germans through the Siegfried Line and back over the Rhine,
not a time to pause and turn west,
even to open Antwerp, for if the larger
attack succeeded Rotterdam would
soon be captured and the Germans in
Le Havre would surely not be able to
hold out for long. Consequently the
decision was taken to forget the
Germans in the west and use the
waiting airborne divisions to seize
bridges to enable ground forces to
advance seventy or eighty miles to
capture an area from which the Siegfried Line could be outflanked. With
that decision the chance of finishing
the war in 1944 was lost.

It is true that Eisenhower early
realised the importance of Antwerp,
for in a directive of the 4th September,
after pointing out that the best way
to defeat Germany was to strike at
the Ruhr and the Saar, he said 'the

mission of the Northern Group of Armies and that part of the Central Group of Armies which is operating north-west of the Ardennes, is to secure Antwerp, breach the Siegfried Line covering the Ruhr and seize the Ruhr.'

One of the criticisms that has been made of Eisenhower is that his orders were not precise enough and it might be said that the above is an example, for 'to secure Antwerp' need not necessarily mean clearing the Scheldt and sweeping the eighty miles of sea and river approaches, although it could be argued that it could not mean anything else, for an Antwerp unable to be used as a port was a liability.

Eisenhower's Naval Commander-in-Chief, Admiral Sir Bertram Ramsay, had clearly realised the importance of Antwerp for on 3rd September, the day before the port was captured, he sent a 'for action' telegram to SHAEF. It stressed the importance of preventing the Germans from carrying out

demolition or blocking the port, from mining and blocking the Scheldt and of capturing the coastal batteries so that the approach channels could be cleared.

Also, at a top level meeting at Versailles on 4th October Admiral Ramsay vehemently condemned 21st Army Group's delay in opening the port. One of those attending was the Chairman of the Chiefs of Staff Committee, Field-Marshal Sir Alan Brooke, who later wrote in his diary that 'for once Monty's strategy is at fault.' Unfortunately, he said nothing at the time.

Eisenhower continued to stress the importance of Antwerp but it was not until well after the failure to seize Arnhem that he made his position undeniably clear. On 9th October he sent a message to Montgomery saying that Antwerp was of 'first importance to all our endeavours' and requesting his 'personal attention'; on 13th October, in reply to Montgomery's

now-famous 'Notes on Command in Western Europe', which pushed very hard for a single land forces commander, Eisenhower pointed out that the real issue was not command at all but Antwerp, Antwerp, Antwerp. At last he issued firm, explicit orders that the port *must* be opened forthwith.

This produced results and on 16th October Montgomery issued orders which left no room for doubt: 'Operations designed to open the port of Antwerp will be given complete priority over all other offensive operations without any qualifications whatsoever.' He expected this to be quickly accomplished and the Reichswald attack was scheduled for 10th November.

But it took nineteen days of some of the hardest fighting of the war before the Germans were cleared from both shores of the estuary and then came the task of sweeping the sea approach, estuary and river. With the loss of only one vessel and crew 267 mines were swept and a number of small ships got through on 26th November. Two days later the first convoy reached harbour safely. Almost immediately huge quantities of war materials funnelled through the great port to the waiting armies, but by now the Germans had been able to stabilize their front in Holland. They would have to be cleared back across the Meuse before an attack on the northern end of their line could be risked.

The responsibility for the decision to postpone the opening of the port of Antwerp lies fairly evenly on Eisenhower and Montgomery. On his part the Supreme Commander frankly admitted it. In a 'personal report' to the Combined Chiefs of Staff on 3rd December 1944, that is before the German attack in the Ardennes, he said that he still considered that delay in capturing Antwerp – 'the effects of which have been felt through-

German prisoners are marched away through Antwerp

Above: Optimistic British troops on a friendly Dutch landscape. *Below:* Liberation: the British pass through Eindhoven. *Right:* Lieutenant-General Brian Horrocks, commander of XXX Corps

out later operations' – was a gamble worth taking. More publicly, in his final published report he wrote, 'I took full responsibility for this and I believe that the possible and actual results warranted the calculated risk involved.'

But in his memoirs, by which time the serious results of the delay were pretty generally recognised, he had

second thoughts and decided that what he had wanted was both the opening of Antwerp and a bridgehead over the Rhine at Arnhem. 'After the completion of the bridgehead operation he (Montgomery) was *to turn instantly and with his whole force* to the capture of Walcheren Island and the other areas from which the Germans were defending the approaches to Antwerp.'

Montgomery, in his memoirs, seems to want the best of all worlds, for he says, first, that the responsibility was

A British platoon parades before mounting guard over the deserted docks

not his but the Supreme Commander's, who did not *order* him to open Antwerp; second, that Eisenhower did not in fact say that he was to concentrate on Antwerp after Arnhem but on the contrary did not give priority to that until 9th October – two weeks later and, lastly, that anyway 'the quickest way to end the German war was not *merely* to have free use of Antwerp but to deliver a hard blow which would finish off the Germans and at the same time give us the ports we needed on the northern flank.' (Author's italics.)

Undoubtedly the delay in getting the use of Antwerp's great port installations had far-reaching effects but it is impossible to be specific about what these were, for the game of 'If only . . .' is particularly futile when applied to war – it is rather like trying to determine the course an avalanche would have taken had a certain stone not been dislodged.

But as far as the crucial battle with which this book deals is concerned I think it fair to say that, if major attention had been given to the task, Antwerp could have been fully operational within ten days to two weeks after its capture. In that case, and assuming that the Arnhem Operation still went exactly as it did, then the attack from the Nijmegen bridgehead through the Reichswald section of the Siegfried Line could have been mounted – just as Montgomery planned after Arnhem – by mid-October. In that case it would probably have quickly reached its objectives for the German troops who, when it was finally launched, slowed it down – mainly three divisions of parachute infantry – were then being re-formed after their near destruction in France and it was another month before they were ready to fight again.

If, on the other hand, as General Horrocks thinks, it would have taken much longer than two weeks to clear the Germans from the Antwerp approaches and the Arnhem Operation had had to be postponed, it probably would not have achieved what it did – the most important seizing of the Nijmegen bridgehead. Speed was the essence of that plan and Horrocks, who commanded the corps concerned, wrote in his memoirs that while there was any chance of bouncing a crossing over the Rhine and cutting off the industrial heart of Germany in September 1944 Montgomery would have been wrong to deflect his resources to a subsidiary task.

It is up to the reader to make his choice.

Frustrations and postponements

Once the restraints imposed by supply shortages were removed it looked as though the time had come for Eisenhower to carry out the second part of the task set him by the Combined Chiefs of Staff – 'to undertake operations aimed at the heart of Germany'. But the pause in the assault which followed the Arnhem operation, during which the Scheldt was cleared and the port of Antwerp opened, went on and the Germans were granted valuable time, just as Hitler had confidently predicted. They used it well: control was regained of the uncontrolled retreat and firm defence lines were established; the economy was moved into total war – surprisingly for the first time – and record arms production achieved; a great manpower comb-out took able-bodied men out of non-fighting jobs and turned them into hastily trained infantry, the *volksgrenadiers*. They were replaced by the lame, the sick and the deaf, some of whom were even formed into second line troops, and by these means part of Germany's staggering losses were replaced.

But Hitler's most important accomplishment during this respite was the creation of a new mobile reserve to replace the one lost in France and the strict husbanding of it for a great offensive, an up-to-date version of the famous blitzkriegs of earlier years. With it he intended to change the whole situation on the Western Front in a matter of days.

For the American and British armies it was a most costly delay.

It had not been intended to let up the pressure against the Germans. On the contrary as early as 3rd September, the day before Antwerp was captured, Montgomery had decided that the time had come when the German collapse might be completed with one hard blow, for it seemed to him that the armies on his front were badly off balance, a state in his enemy which it is always his intention to bring about, and that for them a dangerous gap was opening between their Fifteenth Army on the coast which was being forced north-east and their Seventh Army, whose survivors of the defeat in France were moving east in headlong retreat.

At a meeting in Brussels with Bradley and Hodges (Lieutenant-General Courtney Hodges, commanding First US Army) he proposed ramming British Second Army into this split like a giant wedge. With the airborne troops dropping ahead of the armour and infantry to seize and hold open crossings over the main canals and rivers it should be possible to push XXX Corps all the way to the Nijmegen-Arnhem area. Flank support would be supplied by bringing up a corps on either side and by an attack north-east by First US Army. The plan, named Operation Comet, was to start in three days, on 6th September, and its ultimate object was to outflank the Siegfried Line.

At this time the great bogey which seemed to lie ahead was the famous German West Wall which the Allies, with memories of an unbreachable German defence line in the First World War, called the Siegfried Line. They greatly overestimated its capabilities in the autumn of 1944.

This long line of fortifications had been begun in 1936 by Hitler, when he occupied the demilitarised Rhineland, but had then been no more than a short stretch of many small, mutually supporting pill boxes sited along the Saar River opposite the Maginot Line. Its purpose was to delay any French invasion of Germany. Two years later when Czechoslovakia showed signs of fight Hitler ordered a crash programme to thicken existing fortifications and to extend the line from north of Aachen along the German border to the Rhine and then following that river right down to the Swiss frontier.

The famous 'Autobahn engineer', Fritz Todt, was put in charge and with some 700,000 men, 4,000 concrete

The river Waal

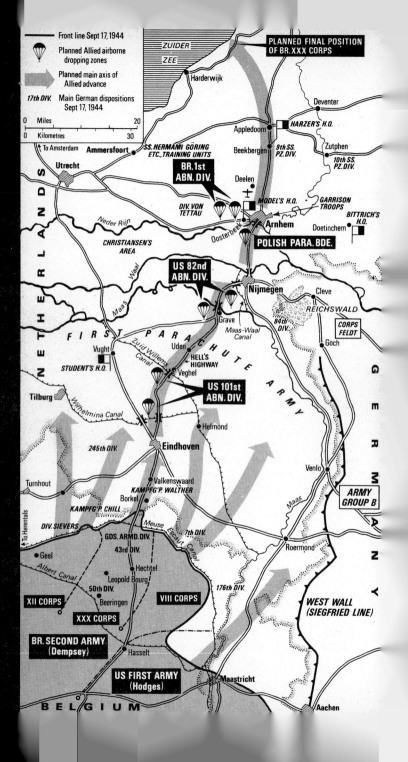

mixers and one-third of all German cement produced, was responsible for building over three thousand pill boxes, bunkers and observation posts in eighteen months. A bit more was added to the West Wall in the next two years and, in 1940, so that their great defence line could never be outflanked as they intended to deal with the Maginot Line, the Germans extended a modified version of the West Wall north from Aachen all the way to Cleve on the Dutch frontier.

But the quick conquest of Holland, Belgium and France and the driving of the British from the Continent apparently rendered the long line of defences obsolete. In 1940 the frontier of the Thousand Year Reich was on Europe's coastline and the West Wall was locked up and abandoned until the extent of the Allied victories in July 1944 forced Hitler to consider its importance. Orders were issued for the great pill-box complexes to be opened (it was said that no one could find the keys) and refitted at maximum speed but, although more than 200,000 workers were rushed there, little could really be done to make the obsolete defences adequate to deal with the heavy tanks, the self-propelled guns, the flame-throwers amd the rocket firing aeroplanes of 1944.

The main value of the West Wall was psychological: it gave the weary, defeated German soldiers falling back an illusion of strong defence and it represented to them their duty to protect the Fatherland. To the equally weary Allied soldiers, who had long heard of its invincibility, it loomed as a fearsome obstacle.

Despite the optimistic forecast of SHAEF Intelligence that the Germans had only fifteen divisions for the defence of the West Wall and 'a further five or six may struggle up in the course of the month making a total of twenty. The West Wall cannot be held with this amount . . .' the pursuing Allied troops were stopped and turned back when they first ran

into it in the Eifel and in the Ardennes.

The alternative to breaking through the Siegfried Line in a costly frontal assault was to turn it, as the Germans had turned the Maginot Line. The place to do this was at its northern end near the Dutch frontier where the Germans had not bothered to extend the fortifications along the Waal to the North Sea after conquering Holland because it seemed inconceivable that any enemy would try to advance into Germany by this roundabout route. And, anyway, the land north of the Reichswald Forest as far as the broad Rhine was polder, recovered from marsh by dykes, not country through which to mount a mechanised attack.

Nevertheless the idea of seizing the general area Grave-Nijmegen-Arnhem with airborne troops supported by land forces and then launching an attack around the end of the Siegfried Line which would turn south-east and strike for the Ruhr seemed perfectly feasible in September because of the apparent German collapse. Eisenhower noted on 5th September, 'The defeat of the German armies is now complete and the only thing needed to realise the whole conception is speed.' This was Montgomery's opinion as well and he quickly resumed the attack even though of the twenty-one divisions under his command only two were in a position to maintain the offensive – the 11th Armoured in the Antwerp area and the Guards Armoured near Louvain.

On 6th September Second British Army's XXX Corps resumed its advance with these two divisions, the Guards aiming for crossings of the Albert Canal, the 11th Armoured trying to break out of Antwerp through the now reinforced northern industrial suburbs.

Surprisingly the Germans, who had seemed to be in uncontrolled retreat, now rallied, turned and fought hard and well to hold the swampy heath between the Albert Canal and the Meuse-Escaut Canal. In one key town,

Army Group commanders Montgomery and Bradley, centre, with two of their army commanders, Hodges of First US Army (left) and Dempsey of Second British Army (right)

Hechtel on the road to Eindhoven, a large part of the Guards Armoured Division's tanks and infantry was stopped and held up for six days by about 850 German parachute infantry with three tanks. The infantry of 11th Armoured Division forced crossings of the Albert Canal north of Antwerp but were unable to reinforce their bridgeheads so the armour could cross and were moved over to XXX Corps' right flank which was exposed because the American armoured division which had been given the job of flank protection was halted for three days by shortage of fuel.

When the Germans holding Hechtel were finally overcome 150 of them were found dead and another 200 wounded, but it was now 12th September and the weather had prevented the airborne operation. Even though the British were now established across the Meuse-Escaut Canal on the borders of Holland it was apparent that Operation Comet was not powerful enough to push a force overland against stiffening German resistance.

But if the ground forces available could not get through there was another army which could and which had been waiting for such an opportunity for weeks – the First Allied Airborne Army. Eisenhower had long wanted to use his airborne divisions in a plan of 'imagination and daring' so that when Montgomery proposed that Comet be greatly expanded into Market-Garden in which all the airborne forces be used to seize six main canal and river bridges simultaneously and to hold them while Second Army's tanks and infantry drove hard and fast through them up a narrow corridor to the northern-most bridgehead at Arnhem, the Supreme Commander responded enthusiastically: 'I must say that it [Operation Market-Garden] is designed not only to carry out most effectively my basic conception with respect to this campaign but it is in exact accordance with all the understandings that we now have.'

'Market' was the airborne part of the operation and 'Garden' the land advance. Three airborne divisions were to be used, the biggest parachute operation of the war. The US 101st Airborne Division's task was to seize bridges and defiles immediately in front of the waiting tanks and infantry, notably bridges over the Zuid Willemsvaart and Wilhelmina canals. The US 82nd Airborne Division were to seize and hold the bridges at Grave on the Maas and at Nijmegen on the Waal (as the Meuse and Rhine are called in Holland). Finally the British 1st Airborne Division were to capture the northernmost position, Arnhem, 'with sufficient bridgeheads to pass formations of Second Army through.'

As is well known the operation did not completely succeed due to a number of unexpected factors but in the two American drop zones opposition came only from 'low-grade troops' on the first day and almost all objectives were seized. The 101st Airborne dropped 6,769 men in half an hour with two per cent casualties and only two units missed their drop zones. The land forces passed through them after a bitter fight south of Eindhoven and pushed on towards Nijmegen and Arnhem.

The next airborne division, the 82nd, 'landed against almost no opposition' and captured the very important bridge over the Maas at Grave, in a dashing *coup de main*, and also secured a bridge over the Maas-Waal canal. But at Nijmegen the chance to seize the thousand foot long road bridge in the first few hours, when it was held by a few low-grade troops, was not taken. There were several reasons which seemed valid at the time, of which the most important was the need to seize first a 300-foot-high land

mass southeast of Nijmegen, the Groesbeek-Berg en Dal, for the bridge could not have been held if the Germans had been occupying this position. Field-Marshal Model had immediately ordered some of a crack SS Panzer Division who, unluckily for the Allies, were re-forming in the Arnhem area, to the Nijmegen road bridge. They arrived within hours of the landing so that when the parachutists moved towards the bridge approach they were not strong enough. It was decided to wait for the Guards Armoured Division to get up to them.

The heaviest concentration of German troops was, quite accidentally, a few miles east of Arnhem where the remains of the II SS Panzer Corps were assembling after their retreat from France and Belgium. German local defence forces were also strong in this area but the crowning bad luck for the attackers was the presence of the commander of German Army Group B, Field-Marshal Model, at Oosterbeek a little more than a mile from where the British were dropping. At his best in emergency situations Model took personal command and rapidly concentrated forces against Arnhem. Soon, as well as the remnants of the two divisions of II SS Panzer Corps, thirteen battalions of infantry, two battalions of panzer grenadiers, three battalions of flak guns, a battalion of heavy mortars and a regiment of artillery had surrounded the men of the 1st Airborne Division.

Despite the utmost heroism and determined fighting on the part of the British – the official German report described it as 'bloody hand-to-hand fighting with cold steel' and admitted losing 3,300 men – the Germans regained the vital Arnhem bridge after four days. But the delay had been of the greatest importance, particularly to the battle for the bridges at Nijmegen, for the entire 10th SS Panzer Division had been ordered to move there and were only prevented from doing so by the gallant stand of the 600 paratroopers who clung to the

north end of Arnhem bridge against attack after attack. The time thus bought allowed the tanks of the Guards Armoured Division to drive through to Nijmegen and reinforce 82nd Airborne's comparatively light forces.

During the night of 25th/26th September the survivors of the drop around Arnhem were ferried across the river. The cost had been very heavy; nearly 8,000 casualties of whom 1,300 were dead and 1,700 seriously wounded; five Victoria Crosses, the rarest gallantry award, were awarded – four of them posthumous. When General Eisenhower learned the full details, including the opinion that 'due to the great losses suffered at Arnhem it will probably not be possible to reconstitute the 1st Airborne Division' he wrote to its commander, General Urquhart: 'There has been no single performance by any unit that has more greatly inspired me or more highly excited my admiration than the nine day action of your Division.'

At Nijmegen, too, the fighting had been hard and bitter after the first day as German reinforcements came in to hold the bridges and others were fed into the Reichswald Forest looming darkly on the flank. A new attempt to storm the highway bridge late during the first night was thwarted by a vigorous German counter-attack which forced the parachutists to withdraw from the narrow city streets and reorganise. A third attempt at 7.45 in the morning of 18th September which tried to come in from the east was stopped by intense small arms, 20mm anti-aircraft and 88mm shell bursts.

Just after dawn of the second day the Germans sallied out of the Reichswald forest, seven to eight miles south-east of Nijmegen, and attacked several of the parachutists' easternmost positions. Some villages were lost and

retaken but the German pressure increased and only the timely arrival of three more battalions who dropped into the Nijmegen circle that afternoon restored the situation. But by this time the Germans' hold on the bridges was so firm it was obvious that they could not be driven off without armour and artillery.

Early the next morning, 19th September, the armoured cars of the Guards Armoured's reconnaissance made contact with the airborne troops and reported that the bulk of the tanks were not far behind and that afternoon General Horrocks and Brigadier Gavin met. The decision was to attack both bridges with mixed assault groups of parachutists, infantry and tanks.

The attack against the railway bridge was stopped some 500 yards short by fire from rifles, machine guns, 20mm anti-aircraft and 88mm dual purpose guns. The point tank was knocked out and the foot driven to cover. The assault against the highway bridge received an even hotter reception and when four tanks were knocked out and the infantry and parachutists had taken many casualties it, too, was called off.

Bad weather prevented any more drops to replace the airborne casualties and the gaps in the line were filled by pressing into service 450 glider pilots. They were courageous to the point of recklessness but individualists to a man who, moreover, had received no training as ground fighters or in tactical organisation and were consequently of little real value.

To break the stalemate the bold decision was taken to ferry a couple of battalions of paratroops across the wide, fast-flowing river in the teeth of the enemy in order to be able to attack the bridges at both ends at the same time. The only craft available were twenty-six canvas and plywood assault craft designed for unopposed crossing of water obstacles. It took longer than expected to

Water barriers, a major obstacle in fast mobile forms of modern warfare evolved during the Second World War. *Above left:* 50th Division troops move up to consolidate the bridgehead over the Escaut Canal. *Below left:* Royal Engineers replace a bridge destroyed by the Germans over the Escaut Canal. *Above right:* A Bailey bridge over the Albert Canal, with refugees moving into the Allied rear areas. *Below right:* 53rd Division troops cross the River Meuse by pontoon bridge

clear the Germans from parts of Nijmegen and it was not until 3pm on 20th September that the parachutists began to wade out in the shallow water and clamber into the frail, nineteen-feet long craft. The crossing was supported by concentrated fire from the tanks' guns and about one hundred artillery pieces. The RAF bombed and strafed the north bank and rocket-firing Typhoons went in against all known German gun positions. Lastly, smoke shells were fired as the boats took to the water but the wind was erratic and the smoke screen ineffective.

This assault made in full view of a dug-in enemy was one of the minor epics of the Second World War and its drama was more like the film variety than the real thing. The boats were swept downstream at ten knots, whirled round and round making some of the men seasick. Some capsized, men were rescued by others diving in for them and one actually walked ashore under water with full equipment. The fire from machine guns, anti-aircraft guns and air bursts from larger pieces was murderous and continuous. Later a survivor described the appearance of the water as the bullets and shell fragments hit it as 'a school of mackerel feeding'. Half the boats got across and each man fought as an individual at first, because the casualties had broken the command links. Firing at every German they saw they charged across open ground under sweeping fire. Over fifty Germans were killed before a diked road nearly half a mile from the river was gained and turned into a temporary defence line.

The thirteen remaining boats were paddled back across the river by their three-men engineer 'crews'. Eleven regained the south bank to be filled immediately with more paratroopers. In all, six crossings were made and most of two battalions got across and

The parachute landings by First Allied Airborne Army

struck out for their objectives one of which was the north end of the railway bridge which they stormed, driving the Germans out. Triumphantly they flew the Stars and Stripes and the example of their remarkable feat of arms inspired the Guards who charged across the bridge with five tanks, lost three but gained the northern end with the remaining two. The parachutists pressed home their attack from both ends and by half past seven of the third day after the parachute drop, both great bridges were in Allied hands.

Over two hundred casualties were sustained by 82nd Airborne, but 267 German dead were found on the railway bridge alone. Allied possession of these bridges, and the bridgehead over the Waal thus made possible, was to have a decisive effect on the war and it has always been something of a mystery that they were not blown. The answer would seem to be that it was Model himself who forbade their destruction because he did not believe that the small Allied forces which had been able to get to Nijmegen could possibly capture the bridges and he expected hourly to regain the Arnhem bridge and unleash the SS Panzer troops, held on the wrong side of the river there, to take back Nijmegen and strongly counter-attack the forces there driving them back across the Maas. He was confident that no force could cross the wide Waal but he could not allow for the exceptional quality of the men of the 82nd Airborne Division whose incredible feat in crossing the river in slow, flimsy boats in broad daylight in full view of a large, well-armed force brought unreserved praise from all who saw it – on both sides.

When the British Second Army commander, General Dempsey met Brigadier-General Gavin, the paratroopers' commander, after this exploit he said, 'I am proud to meet the commander of the greatest division in the world today.'

After the withdrawal from Arnhem

the balance sheet of Market-Garden could be drawn up. In the sense that it fell short of its objectives, particularly the main one, it must be reckoned a failure but it was a failure with important compensations: the German defence of Holland which had been building along the lines of the canals in the south had been completely shattered; their forces had been split in two by the corridor from the Albert Canal to the Waal and although they had counter-attacked it furiously and had even succeeded in cutting it briefly on three occasions, by the time the survivors of the 1st Airborne Division had been withdrawn from Arnhem the rest of the two American airborne divisions had been flown in and the corridor had been made impregnable – at least to any forces the Germans could find for this end of their long line. By seizing the Nijmegen bridges and by vigorously extending the bridgehead and pushing east almost to the German

frontier a base had been established for a subsequent thrust around the Siegfried Line aimed at the Rhine; the bridgehead beyond the Maas would eventually enable an attack to be mounted to clear the west bank of the Rhine opposite the Ruhr; some very valuable airfields in Holland had been gained. Finally, the fact that the Allies now stood on their frontier from the Reichswald Forest to Metz made it impossible for the Germans, desperately short of men and matériel because of the demands of the Eastern Front, to know where the main attack by the Western Allies would fall. A whole new sector now posed a threat.

On the debit side the high hopes for this imaginative and daring enterprise had not been realised. In the realm of high strategy the German army had not collapsed and the Siegfried Line still remained a great barrier. Nor had the main strategic objectives been achieved for the bridgehead at Arnhem, which would

Left: Nijmegen, battered by Allied shelling before the link up between ground and airborne troops. *Above:* Supplies are brought across the River Waal at Nijmegen, despite the bridge being destroyed as the Germans fell back

have enabled an advance to the Zuider Zee and the cutting off of the German Fifteenth Army in Western Holland, had not been established; the Siegfried Line had not been out-flanked; 21st Army Group had not been able to move into position to drive around the north flank of the Ruhr. And the cost had been dear – over 17,000 casualties including 596 pilots and 860 glider pilots, 144 transport aircraft and 88 tanks. Finally the priorities of Market-Garden had meant that Antwerp had remained closed and the Germans had been allowed to entrench themselves on both sides of the Scheldt and it would now take large forces and much bitter fighting

to dislodge them. The Germans had been alerted to the weakness at the northern end of their West Wall and immediately set about thickening the fortifications there and, by controlled flooding creating a barrier farther north.

Perhaps with the benefit of hindsight one can say that it would have been better to have done something else in September 1944 but Market-Garden could well have succeeded and if it had it would have gone down in history as a stroke of genius. Such gambles are always worth taking.

The importance of the Allied gains in Holland was not lost on the Germans. The sixty-five-mile long salient ending with the Waal bridgehead became Hitler's number one priority and he ordered a panzer brigade, a battalion of Tiger tanks, and an anti-tank battalion to reinforce the variegated divisions on the eastern side of the corridor now known as the First Parachute Army and put under

General Kurt Student. Hitler also ordered that two panzer divisions recently withdrawn from the Aachen front be refitted and sent to wipe out the corridor. Nijmegen was described as the 'gateway to the Reich' and the destruction of its bridges was to be accomplished 'at any cost'.

The first attempts came from the Luftwaffe who mounted a number of heavy attacks during the night of 26th/27th September and the following day. But the Allies had hurriedly got Dutch airfields operating and were able to send wave after wave of fighters – over four hundred – to meet the German bombers and forty-six of them were shot down. The attempt to cut the bridges with bombs was called off.

Two days later a dozen frogmen swam down the river at night towing floating mines and managed to attach some to both bridges. Most of these brave men were captured or killed but their mines exploded dropping a span of the railroad bridge into the river and blowing a twenty-five yard gap in the road bridge. Although they had to work under observed artillery fire the engineers immediately put up an emergency bridge supported on barges anchored between the permanent bridges. They also repaired the gap in the road and to guard against any more desperate attempts the river was floodlit, booms and nets laid, anti-tank guns sited along the banks and the whole area constantly patrolled.

Traffic continued to flow north over the bridges to enlarge and reinforce the salient in preparation for a major offensive from it.

After Arnhem Montgomery assessed the Germans' next move. They would first try to destroy, or at least cut, the narrow corridor to Nijmegen while at the same time denying the Allies the use of the Scheldt for as long as possible. They would also try to stabilise their northern front along the line of the Waal and would hold a salient west of the Maas for as long as

possible to keep the Allies off the Ruhr. On his part he never forgot that his prime objective was the Ruhr which meant, of course, that the Rhine had to be crossed in force. This was the objective of the offensive to be launched from the Nijmegen salient and the supporting attack across the Roer which was to follow.

It was hoped to start the first part of this pincer operation, the drive to clear the Reichswald, on 10th October but, as we have seen, on Eisenhower's insistence everything was stopped so that Antwerp could be opened. On 18th October, when this operation was well under way, Eisenhower met Montgomery and Bradley at Brussels and plans for the next phase of the war were decided. In the south 6th Army Group were to advance and cross the Rhine between Basle and Strasbourg; in the centre two of 12th Army Group's three armies, Hodges' First and Patton's Third, were to advance to the Rhine and establish bridgeheads while Bradley's other army, Simpson's Ninth would come under Montgomery's 21st Army Group and be used to attack north-east in conjunction with First Canadian Army's breakout south-east from Nijmegen. The new date for this great pincer attack was to be 10th November.

In the north this was to be done by First Canadian Army with the British XXX Corps under command and after the Reichswald had been cleared and the supporting offensive by Ninth US Army launched across the Roer it was intended that the Canadian divisions would drive north from Nijmegen (while XXX Corps were continuing south-east) to 'secure the high ground between Arnhem and Apeldoorn with a bridgehead over the IJssel river.

Although south-west Holland was cleared by 28th October the Germans launched a strong attack west from the Venlo salient on the day before and it took all available Allied

Field-Marshal Model with members of his staff

38

strength to stop them. The Germans also kept up the pressure against the northern and eastern perimeter of the Nijmegen bridgehead, 'the island' as this area surrounded by floods came to be called.

Nor had the Germans abandoned their attempts to destroy the Nijmegen bridges and so cut off the 'island', the obvious springboard for an attack. Mines were floated down the Waal and some slipped past the boom defences and damaged the barge bridge. A new type of boom put a stop to this but the Germans were desperate and continually tried new ideas right up to the time the offensive was finally launched. One dark January night, for instance, a flotilla of seventeen one-man *Biber* submarines was slipped from towing vessels a mile or so upstream from the easternmost boom. Only three got all the way to within sight of the bridges and two of these were engaged by artillery and one sunk. All the vessels were lost but nine of the daring submariners got back. Most of the others froze to death.

With the success of the German attack across the Maas and the continued pressure in the north Montgomery decided that it would be unwise to try to advance from Nijmegen with both flanks hostile. The Germans had first to be cleared back across the Maas all along its length. Orders were given for this to be done and the Reichswald battle was once again postponed.

By the 9th November an 'international' operation mounted by Canadian, Polish, British and American troops had cleared all Germans from south of the Maas. Control of the Nijmegen salient then passed to Fourth Canadian Army. On the 4th December a set piece attack was launched against the Germans west of the Maas opposite Venlo and five days later almost all of southern Holland south and west of the Maas was clear. The front had been 'tidied up' and it was time to schedule the breakout from Nijmegen through the Reichswald once more.

Another top level conference was held at Maastricht in Holland on 7th December at which once again the question of a reorganisation of the command structure was discussed and argued at length and once again Montgomery did not get overall command of all forces north of the Ardennes. But it was agreed that the main attack would be north of the Ruhr and entrusted to 21st Army Group with Ninth US Army under command.

Just before going to this conference Montgomery met Lieutenant-General Brian Horrocks, the commander of

XXX Corps and discussed the attack from Nijmegen with him.

'How many divisions do you want, Jorrocks?' he asked.

'Seven,' Horrocks replied without hesitation and after the conference with Eisenhower, Montgomery telephoned to say that he would get them and that he should start thinking out the plan of battle in detail. Later that evening Montgomery telephoned the commander of the First Canadian Army, General Crerar, and told him that it would be his army's responsibility to break through the Reichswald position and that he was going to get XXX Corps with five divisions to add to two of his own to accomplish the task. The code name for the operation was changed for the fourth time: it now became 'Veritable' and the date was set for 1st January 1945 – a New Year's present for the Germans.

The situation in the Nijmegen salient had not remained static. The Germans had finally realised that they were not strong enough to destroy the bridges but they had another card to play – the bridgehead

Montgomery, commander of 21st Army Group, confers with his army commanders in February 1945. From the left are Dempsey of Second British Army, Crerar of First Canadian Army, and Simpson of Ninth US Army

area could be very much reduced by flooding; if the built-up banks of the Neder Rijn were breached at a critical moment most of the 'island' could be inundated. On 2nd December, after a period of heavy rain, the Germans blew holes in the dykes and the low-lying land north of Nijmegen slowly began to fill.

The Allies had been well aware of this danger and had made detailed plans to evacuate not only their troops and equipment but civilians

Engineers erect a raft to cross a water obstacle in Holland

and their goods and livestock. After three days the only land still above water was a semi-circle of some three miles radius north of the Nijmegen bridges. As the Allied troops fell back the Germans delivered a sharp local attack against the eastern edge of the shrinking perimeter but were repulsed.

Now it was no longer possible for the secondary attack towards Arnhem and the IJssel valley to take place; instead when the Reichswald Battle began amphibious vehicles would be needed to protect the left flank.

On the 15th December Montgomery

considered his carefully laid plans and was most pleased with them. He wrote to Eisenhower saying that he had issued all his orders for the next big operations – Veritable and Grenade – and he would like the Supreme Commander's assent to his spending Christmas in England with his son. He went on to remind Eisenhower that he'd bet that the war would be over by Christmas 1944 and that the Supreme Commander therefore owed him five pounds.

Eisenhower replied saying that certainly Montgomery should spend Christmas at home but that he wouldn't get his five pounds until Christmas Day. He too was feeling good for he had just learned that the President had sent his name to the Senate for approval for promotion to five-star general.

At dawn on 16th December three German armies, two panzer and one infantry, came out of the mists and advanced against the weakest sector of the whole Allied line, the Ardennes. It was beginning of the Battle of the Bulge, Hitler's last offensive and every other activity except countering it had to be shelved.

Operation Verituble and the Roer Dams

The 'Von Rundstedt Offensive' as the Battle of the Bulge was known at the time, broke First US Army's VIII Corps' front and thrust two main armoured drives toward the Meuse between Namur and Dinant. The 'opposite pole' was Antwerp and once the Meuse had been crossed a supporting attack across Holland by Student's forces was to take place.

But the Meuse was never crossed; the Allies, at first thrown off balance by the violence and surprise of the German attack, later steadied and mounted counter-attacks against the flanks of the salient and when these met a month after the offensive had begun the Germans' last hope of avoiding defeat in the west had disappeared.

There was then nothing left for them to do (other than surrender) but play for time in the hope, forlorn as it was to prove, that the alliance against them would break up. It was perfectly clear to Hitler and to the German High Command that the next move lay with the Western Powers and that, undoubtedly, it would take the form of a great offensive designed to carry their armies deep into the heart of Germany. All were agreed that this would happen; no two senior commanders agreed on where the blow would fall.

This was not surprising for the Allies themselves were not agreed: Patton – whose forces had broken off their offensive in December, turned ninety degrees, and driven in the southern edge of 'The Bulge' – wanted to push his Third US Army due east across the Rhine; Bradley who had lost both his First and his Ninth Armies to Montgomery when the Germans' advance cut his communications and had just got the First back, wanted its counter-attack through the Ardennes and the German Eifel supported. Montgomery, who had moved XXX Corps' infantry divisions

British squad advances behind a smoke screen

into a backstop position between Brussels and Maastricht and sent his only available armoured brigade to hold the Meuse bridges, now, single-purposed as ever, wanted to concentrate all possible strength in the north to outflank the Siegfried Line and cut off the Ruhr.

These opinions were strongly held by strong men who not only believed that they alone had the key to a quick victory but who greatly underestimated the abilities of their fellow-commanders whom they saw more as rivals than partners.

Among the bitterest of these rivalries was that which grew up between two Army Group Commanders, Field-Marshal Montgomery and General Omar Bradley, two of the ablest generals to emerge in the war on the side of the Western Allies but of such different temperaments and experience and holding such different theories of war that when they became equals a clash between them was inevitable. The one thing which could have prevented the worst consequences of their personal conflict – a faith in the military ability of the man who was over both of them – was, unfortunately, lacking.

The full story of the Ardennes Offensive is immensely complicated. (See the author's *Hitler's Last Offensive* for a full account of the battle.) It is only necessary here to look at its effect on the struggle for power in which Montgomery, convinced that if put in supreme command he could quickly finish the war, used every possible means to get himself appointed overall ground commander in western Europe, nominally under Eisenhower but in reality taking the actual prosecution of the war against Germany out of his hands.

If Montgomery could accomplish this his intention was to concentrate as many divisions as could be logistically supported in a single great thrust at and through the primary target, the Ruhr, and thence towards the secondary but ultimate target,

Anti-aircraft battery watch a dogfight in the region of the Albert Canal

Above: Montgomery, lone Briton among an array of American military talent. *Right:* American tanks advance through the forests into Germany

Berlin. Because of logistic limitations the divisions remaining south of the Ardennes would have a static defensive or, at best, flank protection role.

This is, of course, the now well-known 'single thrust' versus 'broad front' argument which has been dealt with at length in many books and which it is not intended to go into here, but one of the results of the Ardennes Offensive was that Montgomery found himself almost accidentally in the position he had long been striving for: commanding four armies ranged opposite that part of the German line against which he wanted to mount his thrust – First Canadian, Second British and Ninth and First US. 'It had taken a major crisis to do what I had been asking for ever since August,' he says in his memoirs.

It had been understood that the

placing of two American armies under Montgomery was a temporary measure and that one army at least would be returned to Bradley as soon as the German threat had been dealt with, that is when the First Army attacking south joined the Third Army attacking north and so pinched out the German salient. (Bradley believed that both armies would be returned to him but Eisenhower had agreed at a conference at Maastricht on 7th December, that is nine days before the German offensive in the Ardennes, that Montgomery's 21st Army Group would have Ninth US Army with ten divisions under command at least for the next phase of the war – the crossing of the Rhine and outflanking of the Ruhr from the north.) But on 28th December when the Ardennes battle was well under control Montgomery and Eisenhower met again and Montgomery, who now felt himself to be in a very strong position, pressed once more for the Ruhr to be designated as the next

objective, for all Allied power to be concentrated to that end and for himself to be given 'full operational direction, control and co-ordination of these operations', that is for Bradley's 12th Army Group to come under his command. These proposals were repeated in a strongly worded letter which told Eisenhower that he must be very firm with Bradley and Patton, that any 'loosely worded statement' from him would be quite useless – power must be specifically delegated not merely co-ordination requested. He warned the Supreme Commander that if all power was not directed against the Ruhr in an offensive directed and controlled by one man then 'we will fail again.'

The row that this caused brought a showdown between Eisenhower and Montgomery with the inevitable result that the idea of a separate overall ground commander was relegated to the might-have-beens of history. Eisenhower took firm control and, after certain revisions, issued his outline plan of operations to his three army group commanders.

The First US Army would return to Bradley's 12th Army Group and as soon as the Ardennes battle was over it and Third US Army would drive in a north-easterly direction to close on the Rhine from south of Düsseldorf to Coblenz. And Ninth US Army, made up to a hefty twelve divisions, would be placed under Montgomery's 21st Army Group which would then launch Veritable and Grenade and close to the Rhine all the way from Arnhem to Düsseldorf. The 6th Army Group, holding the southern half of the Allied line, would remain strictly defensive while the northern half cleared the Rhineland.

In fact Montgomery had got most of what he had wanted for it was also decided that Bradley's 12th Army Group Headquarters would move north for the next phase of operations in order for it and Montgomery's HQ to be able to work closely together in seizing the Ruhr.

For Montgomery the whole Ardennes Offensive had been an aside, 'possibly one of the most interesting and tricky battles I have ever handled' as he put it to reporters early in January. He had very much enjoyed dealing with the German offensive but he had never allowed it to distract him from the main objective, the capture of the Ruhr, and with it Germany's war potential.

On Christmas night, when it looked as though once again the panzer armies were on the rampage and there was even talk of evacuating Paris, Montgomery telephoned to Horrocks, who had been visiting some of his troops holding the Meuse river line, and told him to fly back to England. Not surprisingly XXX Corps' commander was shaken and asked why he was being sacked.

Below: 3rd Armored Division during a pause in the advance through the Ardennes, January 1945. *Right:* 40mm light ack-ack unit on watch in Holland

'Don't be stupid, Jorrocks. I want you to go home and have a rest before the big battle – as soon as we've cleared up this mess.'

Horrocks pointed out that it hardly seemed the time for a commander to leave his troops engaged in a great, turning-point battle.

'This battle is finished – the Germans have shot their bolt,' said Montgomery. It was as good an example as we are likely to find of that cardinal military principle, 'maintenance of the objective'.

But there was another reason why Montgomery sent home the commander of the corps he had chosen for the breakout from Nijmegen besides giving him a rest and an opportunity to perfect his plan for the Reichswald Battle. Some eighteen months earlier while standing in the street in north Africa to watch a German air raid (!) Brian Horrocks had most unluckily received a bullet from a Luftwaffe fighter which entered the top of his chest and came out at the base of his

spine piercing lungs, stomach and intestines. Fourteen months in hospital saw the wounds healed but a persistent infection of the colon caused periodic bouts of high fever which made it extremely difficult for him to work at the tremendous pressure imposed on a corps commander in battle. Montgomery knew all this but he also knew that in Horrocks he had an outstanding general (they had known each other for most of their military lives, had fought in France in 1940 when Horrocks commanded a battalion in Montgomery's division and on the Western Desert where he was a corps commander in Montgomery's Eighth Army) and wanted to make sure that he was 'on the top line' for a battle the result of which might well determine the course of the war.

Montgomery pulled his infantry divisions out of the Ardennes early in January, even before the link-up of the two offensives, and moved them back to Holland. On 10th January he ordered the clearing of the last German salient west of the Maas, the Roermond triangle, and as soon as this had been accomplished XXX Corps were placed under command of the First Canadian Army for Operation Veritable and on 21st January a new date was set for the assault on the Reichswald, the fifth and last, 8th February 1945.

The Ninth US Army, commanded by Lieutenant-General William H Simpson ('Big Simp' in order to distinguish between him and another American general, 'Little Simp'), had particularly distinguished themselves under Montgomery's command during the Battle of the Bulge. They were now made up to twelve divisions for their part of the Battle of the Rhineland, Operation Grenade, an advance northeast from the Roer intended to follow the attack through the Reichswald, Veritable, within a few days. There was, however, a snag, one of the 'neglected objectives' of the war – the dams on the upper reaches of the Roer

which were still in German hands. While the Germans controlled this enormous weight of water poised above the Roer valley it would be suicidal folly for Ninth Army to move a large force across the river.

The story of the dams is a strange one for it seems incredible that it took so long to realise their immense tactical importance. Lying just beyond the heavily fortified Huertgen Forest they first appeared as an objective early in September. Shortly afterwards the US XIX Corps Engineer warned his commander that 'If one or more dams were blown a flood approximately 1,500 feet wide and three feet deep lasting from one to three weeks would extend across the entire corps' front.' Unfortunately, as the dams themselves were in the next corps' area, no action was taken on his report.

October and November saw the most costly infantry fighting of the war for the Americans in north-west Europe as First Army's VII Corps tried again and again to clear the Huertgen Forest, peppered with pill boxes and strong points, thickly mined, and pinpointed by German guns. The main objective was the village of Schmidt on a ridge near the centre. Through here most roads ran and the battles unsuccessfully fought for this forest village practically destroyed two American divisions costing them nearly 11,000 casualties.

The high ground and road centre of Schmidt was the key position for an assault against the Roer Dams and it was because the Germans realised their great importance that they fought with savage ferocity to hold them. But, amazingly, the dams were not part of the American objectives at all, during the terrible battles which waged in the Huertgen Forest.

Gradually their significance was realised by SHAEF's planners but not until mid-December were plans made to seize them by ground assault, although earlier in the latter half of November at General Hodges' request,

SHAEF had asked the RAF's 'dam buster' specialists to bomb them out. November's fogs delayed the first attempt until 3rd December when 190 aircraft started off. By the time they were over the area visibility had once more deteriorated and bomb aimers could not see the targets. No bombs were dropped. Out of 200 bombers who tried the next day only twenty-eight were able to attack. There seemed to be little or no damage and Air Chief-Marshal Harris strongly objected that irreplaceable crews were being wasted in an attempt which could not succeed. But Eisenhower could not allow 9th Army to be held on the Roer because of the damned-up waters and he overrode the RAF's objections and ordered the bombing continued.

On 8th December 200 bombers pressed home an attack against heavy anti-aircraft fire and dropped nearly 800 tons of bombs on the three key dams. Eighteen hits were registered on the biggest, Schwammenauel, but its walls remained intact. Four days later the heaviest attack of all dropped 1,500 tons of high explosive on the ends of the dams, along the tops and deep in the water. The only perceivable effect was a small cut near the land end of one dam. With this final failure the attempt to knock out the dams by bombing was called off. It was a job for the ground forces.

On 13th December First Army's V Corps started two attacks intended to converge in the dam area. On the right the infantry advancing through the Monschau Forest ran head on to a strongly defended crossroads and took many casualties before capturing it. But this was on the day that the Germans launched their great counter-offensive through the Ardennes and part of the assault front included the area from which V Corps' right pincer was attacking. German success left the Americans no alternative but to call off the Roer Dams offensive which had cost 2,500 casualties.

In January, as soon as the Battle of

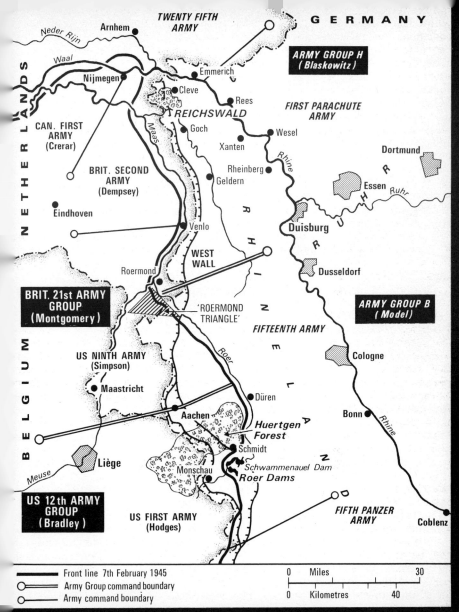

The Roermond Triangle and the Huertgen Forest

Left: German troops wait for the Allied advance at Aachen. Above: Christmas Day 1944. British anti-aircraft unit watch the vapour trails traced above an empty landscape. Below: Artillery attack on the Siegfried Line defences

the Bulge was seen to be won, Eisenhower once again made the Roer Dams the major immediate objective. Bradley accordingly ordered Hodges to capture them but the redeployment of First Army's divisions caused by the Ardennes Offensive meant that it was not until 4th February that the jump-off area, high ground around Ruhrberg and Rollesbroich, was secured and not until three o'clock in the morning on 5th February that the 78th Infantry Division launched the main attack north-east towards the Schwammenauel Dam.

They were supported by a combat command of the 7th Armored Division and by 780 big guns but their progress was disappointingly slow. After seventy-two hours of almost continual fighting against a determined and resourceful German defence they had forced their way into the eastern outskirts of Schmidt and cleared the area between that costly objective and the lake above the dam. This was on the day that Véritable began and two days before Ninth US Army's supporting attack across the Roer was due to be launched. General Hodges, knowing that everything depended upon his forces capturing the dams ordered a fresh division, 9th Infantry, to be passed through the tiring 78th and to capture the Schwammenauel by the next morning. It was a well-nigh impossible task in the time.

The Roer Dams have been called the 'neglected objective' of the Allied campaign in north-west Europe and there seems little doubt that had their importance been realised earlier and priority given to their capture in October and November the course of the war would have been changed. Allied possession of the destructive power of the great mass of water would have prevented the Germans from holding the Roer valley and they would have been forced to fall back to the Rhine. The Germans, of course, realised this full well and for that reason made the holding of Schmidt

and the dams an 'at all costs' task.

The Americans incurred 33,000 casualties in their attempts to clear the Huertgen Forest and as long as Bradley kept First Army short of artillery and new divisions in order that Patton's Third Army could be strongly supported no greater effort could have been made to capture the area which held the key to the Cologne plain and the northern Rhineland. German possession of the Roer dams checked Ninth Army's ability to advance and that, in turn, upset Montgomery's plans for a powerful single thrust north of the Ardennes to capture the Ruhr. It is small wonder that the quip at SHAEF at the time was 'Whose side are you on in this war – Montgomery's or Bradley's?' (Eisenhower Was My Boss: Kay Summersby).

All during the tense fighting of the Battle of the Bulge and the subsidiary German offensive in Alsace which followed it the planners at SHAEF had not forgotten that their own intention was to 'clear the area west of the Rhine, to cross the Rhine and to advance eastward into Germany'. Also, as we have seen, Montgomery never lost sight of these objectives, essential to Allied plans to win the war.

The moment it was possible to do so without endangering the American forces he had withdrawn XXX Corps from their supporting role in the Battle of the Bulge and quickly moved them into position for the breakout from Nijmegen and the clearing up to the Rhine. During the two weeks during which the American First and Ninth Armies were pushing the Germans back from the Ardennes salient Veritable and Grenade were planned in all their complicated details. General Crerar, whose First Canadian Army was to make the main assault, had most of his staff working on the battle plan and all its administrative details. He had entrusted the opening move to Lieutenant-General Horrocks who was confident that with the forces he had been given it would be possible to smash through the Reichswald and move east across the undulating country beyond it in two days. He even hoped secretly to be able to seize a bridge over the Rhine intact.

There were two 'ifs' limiting this optimism though – success depended upon the ground remaining frozen rock-hard and Ninth Army's supporting attack protecting his right flank and keeping the German mobile reserve occupied.

In his planning of the twin offensives Montgomery expected that the Germans, once their main defences had been breached, would fall back to the Rhine. He would be pleased if they did not but instead offered battle west of that river for he knew that the Allies possessed overwhelming superiority in men and matériel coupled with air dominance and that any such stand in the open could only result in the destruction of the remaining German forces.

Canadian troops of the Queen's Own Rifles patrol near Nijmegen in conditions similar to home

But for their part the Germans were determined not to fall back to the Rhine but to hold the Allies along the Siegfried Line. There were many reasons for this decision but the one which persuaded the German commanders to agree with their Führer this time about 'yielding no ground' was that the Rhine was much more than a barrier. It was the main communications artery along which the Ruhr's coal and steel could now be moved. Once the Allies were within sight of the west bank they could stop this traffic and Germany's ability to continue the war would be seriously curtailed. The approaches to the Rhine would be defended with all the ferocity and determination German soldiers defending the Fatherland could summon up – and that, as the Allies had learned to their cost since September – was still a great deal.

But the Allies had no choice but to use the initiative they had regained and to resume the offensive. Eisenhower ordered that, excepting only the capture of the Roer Dams, Operation Veritable and Operation Grenade were designated 'first priority tasks'.

The attack is launched

A great offensive in modern mechanised warfare is an operation of such complexity that no individual or small staff can control, or even understand, all its details. Once the strategic decision has been taken, tactical objectives clearly defined and forces allocated, the responsibility for seeing that the right people are in the right place at the right time with the right equipment is shared among many branches of the services. The chain of command is more like a pyramid built of many smaller pyramids and the man at the top of each is on his own. A major miscalculation or omission on his part can upset, slow down or even stop the gigantic, delicately-balanced war machinery.

Movement, supply and communications on a vast scale begin long before battle is joined and have to continue all through the fighting. Historians, aware of what readers want, tend to do little more than nod appreciatively towards this side of war concentrating instead on the end result. Thus we are told that after a long opening barrage the assault troops move forward as it lifts and attack the prepared defensive positions, perhaps having to call in special weapons or air support before being able to break through, seize their objectives and consolidate.

But for the plan to go like this thousands of soldiers have to be moved unobtrusively to the assault area, have to be supplied and fed there and, once the advance has begun, have to be kept supplied with ammunition, fuel and food, replacements for their casualties and reinforcements when necessary. The wounded have to be dealt with quickly and efficiently and prisoners of war moved back.

Of course it didn't always go like clockwork. Sometimes the services failed and ammunition ran dangerously low or fuel shortage cut mobility or men went hungry but in most fighting advances in north-west

Canadian Army smoke machines in operation in Holland

Europe in 1944 and '45 somehow the bullets and shells, the petrol and oil, the food – and the hardly less essential tea or coffee – appeared more or less when and where they were expected. Somehow roads carried more traffic, lorries bore heavier loads, drivers drove longer hours than had been thought possible. Time and again during the Battle of the Reichswald the 'impossible' was accomplished and 'impassable' roads passed.

The build-up for this largest Allied offensive since the Normandy landings was awesome in its magnitude. Before the enormous bulk of supplies or thousands of troops could be moved into their pre-offensive positions the railways, roads and bridges – and in Holland there always seems to be a bridge just ahead – had to be repaired, strengthened and maintained. The roads were going to have to carry many times the traffic they had been built to bear and as long as the temperature remained below freezing this was quite possible – for a short period. But nine days before the battle, at the time when the traffic was at a peak, there came a sudden thaw. The overburdened routes collapsed and the engineers were faced with an immensely difficult problem.

Fifty companies of them, twenty-nine companies of Pioneers and three road construction companies worked round the clock to shore up and rebuild four hundred miles of roads and to construct one hundred miles of new roads. Nearly a hundred new bridges - including railroad bridges over the Maas – were built. Hundreds of trains and some 35,000 road vehicles strictly controlled by a 1,600-man strong special traffic office kept the supplies moving up to the forward dumps.

On the day before the battle the Deputy Director of Supply and Transport at First Canadian Army HQ was able to report that enough fuel had been brought forward to carry XXX Corps for 150 miles with 'holdings', that is, reserves immediately available, for another 150 miles and 200

miles for Canadian II Corps who were designated for the second phase.

Great importance was placed on the effect of the tremendous opening barrage to be delivered from 1,050 pieces to which were to be added just before the attack, the combined fire power of four divisions. To keep all this going over half a million rounds of 350 different types were moved up to the gun sites. As General Crerar put it to war correspondents the day before the battle their total weight was 'equivalent to the bomb-drop of 25,000 bombers.'

Supplies of many different kinds had to be found from anaesthetics and blood plasma to 8,000 miles of four different kinds of cable. 10,000 smoke generators had to be added to the standard table of smoke stores because of the necessity of concealing the movement of amphibious vehicles. Astronomical numbers were commonplace: 1,000,000 gallons of fog oil, 750,000 maps, 500,000 aerial photographs.

As the battle formations and their supporting troops moved into the constricted assembly area the concentration of mouths to feed placed a great strain on the quartermaster's department. Nevertheless the final figure for food in the forward dumps reached nearly two and a third million rations – Napoleon would have approved.

All this movement and preparation had to be carried out without alerting the Germans to the coming assault and many and elaborate were the means used to mislead them. During daylight hours movement along the roads and rails was kept to the rate established for weeks past and convoys were moved off the roads and camouflaged. As soon as night fell the roads became one long line of vehicles. Dummy gun positions were created of a standard which would ensure that expert examination of photographs would reveal that they *were* dummies. Then in the forty-eight hours before the battle they were replaced by identical real guns. Wireless traffic and other inter-unit communication was kept going at the same rate as in the previous month, the soldiers holding the front line and in forward posts were the same Canadian nfantry who had been there for over a month and in the same numbers. Patrolling and reconnaissance continued as normal except that reconnaissance parties often consisted of high-ranking British officers from the divisions who were to make the attack, wearing Canadian battle dress – which was of a slightly different colour from British – and without any unit identification at all.

At the same time as preparations for Veritable were being carried out in earnest, bogus activity on two other fronts was designed to confuse German intelligence. West of Nijmegen

Below: A convoy rolls towards Germany
Left: Antwerp comes back into action

along the Waal and lower Maas traffic was increased during daylight and wireless messages gave the impression that the troops there were being reinforced. The logical assumption was that the Allies were about to advance towards Utrecht and Amsterdam. Farther south, on the British Second Army front everything was done to convince any watching eyes (and the Germans had many friends in Holland) that the next offensive would be launched from the Roermond area.

We now know the result of all these security measures and attempts at deception: the dummy gun positions in the Nijmegen area had been spotted, as well as some of the camouflaged dumps and troop concentrations but the Germans were well aware of the deviousness of the British and on 5th February the Chief Intelligence Officer at Rundstedt's Headquarters sent a memorandum to key staff officers of Army Group H, holding the German

Left: General Blaskowitz. *Above:*
General Meyer consults Field-Marshal
Rundstedt

right from the North Sea to just north
of Düsseldorf, telling them that
'Allied activities west of the Reichswald are intended to deceive us
regarding the real centre of gravity of
the coming attack. It is possible that
a subsidiary offensive by the Canadians in the Reichswald area might be
launched to draw our reserves but the
appreciation that the main British
attack will come from the big bend
in the Maas is being maintained.' On
the situation maps at the headquarters of the Commander-in-Chief
West the British XXX Corps was
labelled 'whereabouts unknown'.

However German officers nearer the
scene were not convinced that what
was going on around Nijmegen was
only intended to deceive them. General Schlemm, now commanding First
Parachute Army, although assured by
Army Group H's new commander,

General Blaskowitz, that 'there was
no evidence of large enemy concentrations in the Nijmegen area', expected the Allied 'big blow' to come
through the Reichswald and quietly
edged part of his 7th Parachute
Division away from the area they were
holding opposite British Second Army
and moved them to Geldern at the
southern end of the second defence
line east of the Reichswald.

On the Allied side the vast, meticu-
lously planned build-up continued
until by the evening of 7th February
there lay, just behind the Canadian
troops manning the forward positions
between Nijmegen and the dark mass
of the Reichswald, some 200,000 men
with their full complement of guns,
tanks and other weapons backed up
by air support 'on the maximum
scale'. These included heavy bombers
of the RAF Bomber Command and the
US 8th Air Force, medium bombers of
the 2nd Tactical Air Force and fighter
bombers of two RAF Groups and of the
US 9th Air Force. Everything was

ready for a series of tremendous blows, first by bombs, then by massed artillery and finally by overwhelming strength on the ground, which were designed to shatter the end of the Siegfried Line and to debouch on to the Rhineland plain.

The plan, which had undergone many changes since its initial place in the outflanking of the Siegfried Line which was to follow the Arnhem Operation, was in the end largely worked out by General Horrocks and his XXX Corps planning staff. His directive from General Crerar, who had divided Veritable into distinct phases, was certainly straightforward enough: 'To clear the Reichswald and secure the line Gennep–Asperden–Cleve'.

As the Reichswald Siegfried Line was thought to be most formidable Horrocks' XXX Corps was made up to five divisions. The actual decision about which forces to use in the initial assault had been left to Crerar by Montgomery, but as the Field-Marshal had specified that when 21st Army Group closed on the Rhine he wanted the Canadians on the left, the British in the centre and the Americans on the right, there really was no choice but to give the attack through the Reichswald to XXX Corps.

Understandably this did not please Lieutenant-General G G Simmonds whose II Canadian Corps would at first be required to do no more than flank protection. As soon as he received the outline of the proposed battle he wrote to Crerar drawing attention to the 'unfortunate situation which would develop' if no Canadian regiments took part in the initial attack. Probably as a result of his protest, first the 3rd and later the 2nd Canadian Infantry Division were added to Horrocks' forces and given a role in the opening phase. After the Reichswald had been cleared these divisions would revert to II Canadian Corps who would then exploit the left.

German prisoners are marched in

PLASMOLEN 5.-
GROESBEEK 10
NIJMEGEN 19
VENLO 43
MAASTRICHT 114
Roermond 66 km
Venlo 43 km

Spitfires are armed and fuelled for action on a Dutch airfield

With floods on both flanks there was, Horrocks decided, 'no room to be clever' – it would have to be a frontal assault against a well-fortified position, a situation which few commanders would choose. But with almost unlimited air support and the great weight of artillery it should be possible to hammer the defenders into the ground, destroy their communications and smash their defences. Then three infantry divisions supported by two armoured brigades would roll forward in a solid wall over and through the dazed German survivors before they had a chance to reorganise.

But the essence of the battle would be speed, for the initial wave must be through the Reichswald and in possession of the fortified towns on the other side before the German mobile reserve could be brought into battle – if these reached the Siegfried Line defences before XXX Corps broke through them, the task of doing so would become very difficult and very

costly. Even if the Germans were not able to reinforce the Siegfried defences but still succeeded in getting into Cleve and Goch before these places could be captured then the advance to the Rhine could not continue until they were eliminated and that, too, would be a long, costly operation.

Considering all this Horrocks reluctantly decided that the ring-fortified towns that lay across his axis would have to be 'taken out' by bombers the night before the battle. It was not an easy decision for a humane man to take but the mathematics were remorseless – '. . . it was going to be a race between the 15th Scottish Division and the German reserves . . . and all the German reserves would have to pass through Cleve. If I could delay them by bombing it might make all the difference to the battle. And after all the lives of my own troops must come first, So I said "yes".' (*A Full Life:* Lieutenant-General Brian Horrocks.

One of the disadvantages of using heavy bombs in front of a force intending a swift advance is that cratering

can cause long delays particularly in country where the roads are few and have soft ground on either side. For this reason Horrocks asked for incendiaries and anti-personnel bombs to be dropped on Cleve. However the RAF warned that the concrete installations of the Siegfried Line fortifications just west of Cleve could not be dealt with unless the heaviest 'blockbusters' were used and these would produce deep craters. Horrocks agreed to accept unavoidable cratering but specifically asked that the area through which the main Nijmegen to Cleve road ran for the last four miles or so was subjected to airburst bombs only.

The task of the air force extended to pre-battle attacks designed to knock out bridges, railways and ferries behind the breakthrough sector in order to hinder the deployment of reserves and to destroy as many German dumps of fuel and ammunition as possible. But, of course, too great a bombing concentration beforehand would reveal the area to be attacked so other raids had to be made behind the Germans opposite

British Second Army. At the last moment heavy bombers would try to knock out the bridges over the Rhine at Wesel and Emmerich.

Once battle had been joined No. 84 Group RAF would operate as close support for the ground forces, providing reconnaissance, attacking German headquarters, communications and ammunition reserves, and keeping a 'cab rank' of fighter bombers always in the sky ready to go in at once against accepted targets. No. 83 Group RAF would deal, as soon as the battle had begun, with any counter-effort the Luftwaffe might make and, at the same time, concentrate on destroying the communications in the German rear areas.

During the night before the battle the towns of Cleve and Goch were to be completely destroyed and the smaller towns of Emmerich, Calcar, Üdem and Weeze heavily bombed.

As soon as the last bomber had left the area over the battlefield the massed guns of the artillery were to begin their 'programme' with concentrated fire on carefully pre-selected targets in the path of the intended advance. In its closing stages this tremendous barrage would be increased when the four divisions concerned brought in the fire of their tank guns, anti-tank guns, mortars and machine guns in a 'Pepper Pot' saturation of the ground in front of them.

After five and a half hours the barrage would begin to lift and the waiting troops, with Spitfires and Mosquitos flying in overhead, would begin their advance.

Because of the flooding the initial assault front was only some five miles wide. It ran along high ground from just west of Wyler south through Groesbeek to just east of Mook. Into this narrow neck of land between the floods were crammed four infantry divisions and two armoured brigades. From left to right, that is from north to south, these were: 2nd Canadian whose troops were also spread all along the attack front in their

Artillery: the barrage for Reichswald was the heaviest of the war on the Western Front. *Above:* British 5.5-inch gun. *Below:* 7.2-inch gun crew manhandle their gun into position. *Above right:* 155mm Canadian gun under camouflage. *Below right:* Canadian Bofors gun is hauled into position

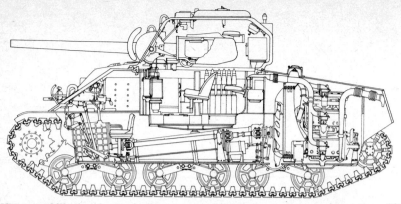

The Western Allies' mainstay in the armoured field soon became the American M4 Sherman tank after the entry of the United States into the war. Though not so well-armed and armoured as the later German tanks, the Sherman packed a considerable punch and was capable of taking a fair amount of punishment itself, though its speed and manoeuvrability enabled it to evade the attentions of more ponderous German tanks. *Crew:* 5. *Weight:* 71,900 pounds. *Armament:* one 75mm M3 gun with 89 rounds and two .3-inch machine guns (plus optional .5-inch machine gun on turret roof). *Maximum speed:* 29mph *Range:* 150 miles. *Armour:* 12mm to 76mm

'normal' positions; then 15th Scottish supported by 6th Guards Tank Brigade, charged with the left-hand attack; then 53rd Welsh who, with part of 34th Armoured Brigade, were to advance right through the centre of the Reichswald and finally, on the right, 51st Highland, with the rest of 34th Armoured Brigade, whose task was to clear the south-west corner of the forest and to open the Mook–Goch road as far as Gennep.

Because the bulk of their troops would be tied down in their front line positions until the assault troops moved through them when the barrage lifted 2nd Canadian Infantry were given a limited first day task – the capture of two villages, Wyler and Den Heuvel and the clearing of the Nijmegen–Cleve road to just short of the Siegfried Line.

The left flank of XXX Corps was held by 3rd Canadian Infantry Division forced by the floods, which extended south from the Rhine lapping the Nijmegen–Cleve road, to face northeast. They were not scheduled to move until 6.0pm on the first day when, with the help of specially adapted vehicles

of the 79th Armoured Division, 'The Funnies', they were to move across the flooded polder, capture the marooned villages and clear up to the south bank of the river.

The three British divisions chosen to make the attack and the two in reserve were all Territorial Army formations and included some of the most famous names in British military history, regiments whose battle honours extended from Marlborough's campaigns through the Napoleonic Wars and the bloody battles of Victoria's reign to the wholesale slaughter of the First World War.

The British method of raising forces for war was influenced by the example of the Roman Legions who were models for four hundred years and then by that of the Germanic tribes the Jutes, the Angles, the Saxons, who filled the vacuum the retreating Romans left. The Roman Legions were recruited from the ends of the earth and Legionnaires differed from one another in race, language and religion. Since there was no common ground for loyalty it had to be created by the adoption of a symbol which was

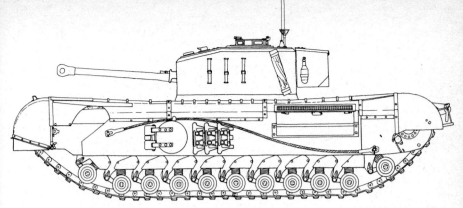

The Infantry Tank Mark 4, named Churchill, was a very successful type, designed for support of and co-operation with infantry. With this in mind, the vehicle was fitted with heavy armament, considerable firepower but only a medium top speed. As with all other tanks, the firepower was augmented very much during the war (the Mk 1 Churchill had a 2-pounder gun, the Mk 8 a 95mm howitzer). Specification for Churchill Mk 7. *Crew:* 5. *Weight:* 40 tons. *Armament:* one 75mm QFSA gun and two Besa 7.92mm machine guns. *Engine:* Bedford Flat Twin Six, 350hp. *Range:* 90 miles. *Maximum speed:* 12½mph. *Armour:* 25mm to 152mm

not connected with any one group and could therefore be fiercely adopted and protected by all – the standard. On the other hand among the tribes the unit came from a district and its members were bound to each other by the powerful bonds of kinship, friendship and shared familiarity and memories.

The Legion model has become the special force – the RAF, SAS and the Commandos; the Germanic tribes military formations became first the county regiments and later the regional divisions: the 15th Scottish, the 43rd Wessex, the 51st Highland, the 52nd Lowland and the 53rd Welsh. All these were to take part in the battle of the Reichswald.

When all was ready the forces lined up on the start line totalled 50,000 troops supported by 500 tanks and some 500 specially adapted tracked vehicles. In addition there were another 10,000 fighting men waiting to strike north-east to secure the left flank and another 15,000 first line troops in reserve with over 500 more tanks.

Facing this mighty force were stretched two German infantry regiments and one of parachute infantry – about 8,000 men. A third infantry regiment 3,000 strong guarded the German right from Kranenburg to Donsbruggen.

The infantry belonged to the 84th Division, one of two which made up LXXXVI Corps which in turn was the right hand half of First Parachute Army. First Parachute was at full strength and of comparatively high combat value at a time when the *Wehrmacht* was scraping the bottom of the manpower barrel. Together with Twenty-fifth Army on the right it formed Army Group H charged with protecting the critical German north flank.

The First Parachute Army was commanded by General Schlemm – a veteran of the desperate fighting on the Eastern Front and a master of the difficult art of conducting a fighting withdrawal. His responsibility extended from the Rhine at Millingen down to Roermond on the Maas and he thus had to be prepared for the Allied 'big blow' to come against either end of his front. As we have seen he opted for the northern end and although he had to keep his 180th Infantry Division deployed along the Maas he edged part of his reserve 'unofficially' north into the Geldern area. He had also been able to persuade the Army Group Commander, General Blaskowitz, who, like himself had only been appointed on 28th January, to let him have one regiment from Twenty-fifth Army's 2nd Parachute Division, his right-hand neighbour, to thicken up the Reichswald defence.

Behind the parachute infantry and grenadiers in the first-line defence blocking the way to Cleve and Goch 84th Infantry Division's commander,

A 240mm gun is checked before an action

Major-General Fiebig, had to be content with a small unit of elderly men normally employed in guarding static installations from saboteurs and the *Magen* (Stomach) Battalion of men with severe chronic stomach ailments necessitating special diet.

Materially too the Germans were at a great disadvantage for the Luftwaffe was no longer able to oppose the Allied Air Force and there was no armour in the Reichswald and only one hundred artillery pieces. Fiebig had thirty-six self-propelled anti-tank guns to oppose the 4–500 tanks which would take part in the initial three main attacks. Reserves available at short notice were a division of parachute infantry and one of panzer grenadiers and the remnants

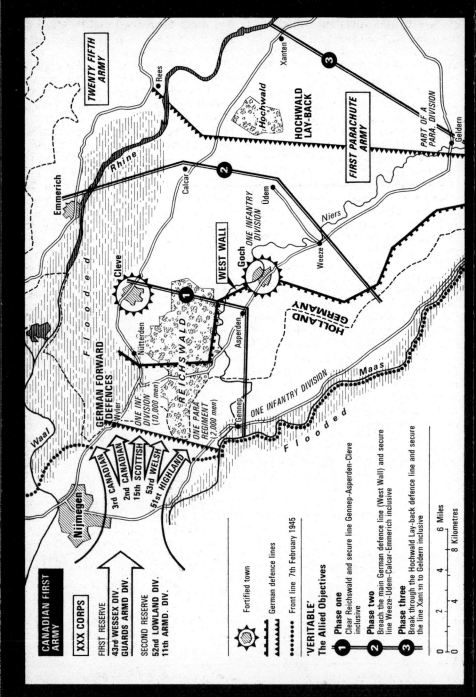

The aims of Operation Veritable

of two panzer divisions which had been brought to the verge of annihilation in the Ardennes Offensive. These could bring about fifty tanks into battle fairly quickly.

There were certain things which would partly redress the balance: although most of the German soldiers were green they were also fresh; they would be fighting on their own soil which always made a great difference to German morale; their panzers and self-propelled guns were greatly superior to Allied tanks. (The difference between a Tiger with an 88mm gun and a Sherman with a 75mm is roughly the difference between a rifle and a shotgun.) Lastly the German defenders had three important natural advantages: the roads were few and narrow, many were unsurfaced; the forest was impenetrable to tanks; floods protected their flanks and the thaw could not have come at a better time.

Allied Intelligence had made a pretty accurate assessment of the German forces in the Reichswald and the available reserves and the night before the battle found General Crerar and Lieutenant-General Horrocks quietly confident about the way it would go. The sudden thaw had been a severe blow – when the ground had been frozen cement hard Horrocks had had 'no doubt at all that we should break out very quickly into the plain beyond and I had hoped secretly to bounce one of the bridges over the Rhine,' but the prospect of heavy going had changed all that. Now there would be no sudden overwhelming victory but progress would continue steadily and it was not possible that the Germans would be able to put up much of a defence when the enormous weight of bombs, shells, men and tanks fell on them.

As the light faded on 7th February the waiting bombers were loaded and the gunners went over their finely-timed fire plan for the last time. The troops assigned to the initial assault checked their weapons and equipment, ate a hot meal and then most of them got down for a good night's sleep for the attack was not scheduled until 10.30 the following morning.

At five o'clock in the morning, in the pitch dark, they were blasted out of their blankets by the noise of the opening of the heaviest barrage employed by the British during the Second World War. From farthest back 122 field guns of large calibre – 155mm, 7.2-inch, 8-inch and 240mm – sent their huge shells crashing into the most solid German defences; the second line of guns consisted of 280 4.5-inch and 5.5-inch; then came 72 3.7-inch anti-aircraft and 576 25-pounders.

The noise was almost unbearable and many of the rear area troops near the guns were deafened for hours. Even far forward the ground shook continuously, buildings vibrated, tent walls whipped in and out with the waves of concussion and everything loose rattled. Speech was impossible and men felt as if they were being hammered into the ground. The sky seemed to be a solid pattern of tracer and there was enough light from the gun flashes to read by.

As well as this intensive bombardment of the German batteries and mortars, command posts and communications, fortifications, houses and localities in the path of the intended advance, the divisions had formed their own 'Pepper Pot Groups' to keep the front under such intensive fire that no deployment to resist an attack could take place. 60 Sherman tanks, 24 17-pounder anti-tank guns, 80 4.2-inch mortars, 114 Bofors, 188 medium machine guns and 12 32-barrel rocket projectors poured their fire on to the immediate front turning it into an almost continual line of explosions.

Confidence ran high as the waiting infantry saw and heard the tremendous barrage for surely few of the defenders would be able to survive that raging inferno. Even the experienced men agreed that it ought to be a walkover.

But it was not.

The first day

Not until the night before his offensive was to be launched did General Crerar move his Tactical Headquarters up behind the assault front, for to have done so earlier would have alerted the Germans. He had left the tactical direction of the first phase of the battle in the hands of Horrocks and shortly after the massed guns of the opening barrage shattered the night Horrocks arrived at his command post which was a platform that the engineers had built for him half-way up a large tree.

It was still dark but the red glow of the guns right across the horizon behind, the pattern of tracer in the sky and the flashes of the shells exploding almost continuously all along the front gave the scene a grim illumination. As soon as the grey dawn came Horrocks was able to see over a good deal of the battle-field that his divisions were waiting to attack.

He had taken great care to try to ensure that reports from the forward units got back to him as quickly and directly as possible. The Signals had run cables up from wireless-link vehicles at the base of his tree command post so that as well as receiving a running commentary on the battle he could speak directly with his commanders. For more complicated orders, or where reasons of security made it desirable, liaison officers with jeeps were also standing by.

A large map of the whole front showed each division's first day objectives: on the right the 51st Highland, limited by their restricted jump-off frontage to advancing one brigade up, were aiming to seize high ground just inside the forest; in the centre where the going was particularly boggy and mine fields were thought to be extensive, the 53rd Welsh, with the help of the special mine-exploding flail tanks of the 79th Armoured Division, were to

Crocodile flamethrower in support of infantry in St Joost

advance one of their infantry brigades into the forest as far as the Brandenberg Ridge; on 53rd's left the 15th Scottish Division, strongly reinforced, were to launch a two-brigade attack as far as the Siegfried defences, pass the third brigade group through to breach that line, and continue into Cleve with the first two brigade groups.

The forest itself was a formidable obstacle of mixed blocks of young trees and older ones interspersed with thicket and scrub. The blocks of geometrically planted trees were separated by long, straight rides which offered an excellent field of fire for a defender. Because of their narrowness some tracks would have to be allocated solely to returning traffic – ambulances, emptied supply vehicles and the like. A few rides were metalled to carry the big logging trucks but the surface of most was sand which could only support tanks if frozen hard. The whole area was, of course, completely familiar to the Germans.

On the left of the British attack into the Reichswald the 2nd Canadian Infantry Division were to use two battalions to cut the main road from Nijmegen east of Wyler and to turn back and capture that place with half their force while the other half moved quickly east to link up with 15th Scottish's left wing. Also, at the end of the first day, when it was expected that the whole Allied line would have moved forward some two or three miles, the 3rd Canadian Infantry Division, carried by the special vehicles of the 79th Armoured Division, would mount an attack north-east across the flooded polder to the Rhine to secure XXX Corps' left flank.

The 79th Armoured Division was a most unusual formation. Although it was the only all-armoured division in the British Army it did not possess a single standard tank. Instead it was equipped with a strange collection of specially adapted tracked vehicles known irreverently as 'the Funnies'.

The most important of these were 'Crocodiles', Churchill tanks equipped for flame throwing; 'Crabs' or 'Flails', Sherman tanks equipped with a device for beating the ground ahead with whirling chains to explode mines;and Armoured Vehicles Royal Engineers (AVREs) which were Churchill tanks equipped with a variety of devices for use by specially trained Assault Regiments of engineers. The most aggressive of these was the 'Petard' which flung a heavy high explosive charge, known as a 'flying dustbin' against concrete walls, snipers' posts, sandbagged houses or emplacements, with devastating effect. Other AVREs carried small box girder bridges which were dropped ahead of them, or 'fascines', bundles of wood up to eight feet in diameter for filling in ditches; some were equipped with 'Bobbins' on which were wound coir and tubular-scaffolding carpets for laying a track over mud for wheeled vehicles. All these tanks were equipped with guns and so could be used offensively, but there were very useful unarmed vehicles as well, 'Kangaroos', a tank with turret removed for carrying infantry forward under small arms fire or shelling; 'Buffaloes', amphibious, tracked vehicles which could carry twenty-four infantry or a 17-pounder or 25-pounder gun or a small infantry carrier; 'Terrapins', the British version of the DUKW, a large, amphibious, wheeled vehicle for carrying infantry or supplies across water; and the 'Weasel', a smaller (half-ton capacity) American amphibious tracked vehicle.

For 3rd Canadian Division's assault against the 'island' villages dotted across the floods, 79th Armoured supplied 114 Buffaloes, equipped with both machine-guns and bazookas, as well as Terrapins and Weasels. The 79th's Crocodiles, Flails and AVRE Petards went in with the three British infantry divisions.

The pre-assault went as planned except that rain and low cloud prevented 325 of the 769 heavy bombers from dropping their bombs on their first-choice targets. Cleve, the mediaeval town from whence had come Henry the Eighth's fourth wife Anna in 1540, was the worst hit. Nearly 1,400 tons of bombs reduced the centre and southern area to heaps of rubble, smashed buildings and killed or wounded many civilians although the fortified cellars stood up remarkably well to the 12,000 pound bombs. Goch was hit considerably less heavily than intended but 500 tons of bombs caused considerable damage to the little town. Here German night fighters made one of their now rare appearances and pursued the Lancasters as far as Brussels, where they shot down two. Ninety-five Stirlings and Halifaxes dropped some 150 tons of bombs on the smaller towns of Calcar, Üdem and Weeze.

After two and a half hours every gun suddenly stopped firing. The silence seemed unreal. Smoke was then fired and the front blanketed to persuade the Germans that the infantry had begun to advance. The surviving German gunners took the bait and fired their high-explosives shells into the smoke. From 7.40am to 7.50 the positions of the German batteries were pinpointed by sound and flash rangers. The counter fire that then followed was so devastating that when the Allies put down smoke again at 10am the German gun crews remained in their shelters and the assault infantry was able to move quickly through the Canadian forward positions right up to the edge of the barrage.

It had begun to rain, a cold penetrating rain that was to fall with only one or two breaks for the next five days creating conditions of the utmost misery for the infantry, turning the low ground into a quagmire and, by increasing the depth of the floods, covering the roads with up to two feet of water.

For the last half hour of the barrage the shelling was brought in from the German middle and rear areas and concentrated on their forward

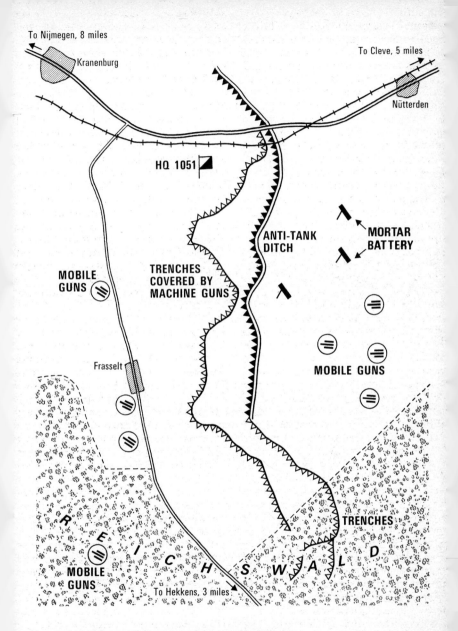

To Nijmegen, 8 miles

Kranenburg

To Cleve, 5 miles

Nütterden

HQ 1051

MORTAR BATTERY

ANTI-TANK DITCH

MOBILE GUNS

TRENCHES COVERED BY MACHINE GUNS

MOBILE GUNS

Frasselt

REICHSWALD

TRENCHES

MOBILE GUNS

To Hekkens, 3 miles

Also: Anti-aircraft guns, light mortars, dugouts and barbed wire

Above: An Alligator crosses the Maas river. *Below:* Allied ingenuity in adapting tanks embraced several kinds of 'funnies' including those shown with a lowering bridge and wooden fascines

positions. At H-hour, 10.30, yellow smoke signalled the first 300-yard lift and the infantry started forward keeping as close as possible to the line of bursting shells. As they reached the forward German positions the effects of the long bombardment were obvious: dazed prisoners told interrogators of the complete disruption of communications, of panic and the breakdown of discipline as the conviction grew that they had been abandoned and were about to be overwhelmed.

We will look at the progress of the offensive from the Allied left to right, that is from north to south: on the northern flank the two Canadian battalions of 2nd Infantry attacked side by side eastwards from the Wyler-Groesbeek road. On the left the Calgary Highlanders, on the right a French-Canadian unit, Le Régiment de Maisonneuve. In order to surprise the Germans entrenched in Wyler facing north-west the Calgary Highlanders did not attack along the direct approach from Nijmegen but bypassed Wyler coming in through the village of Vossendaal and cutting the main road half a mile behind the German position. At the same time the French-Canadian infantry on their right moved quickly eastwards into the village of Den Heuvel, where they found forty-six dead Germans, and on to Hochstrasse on the main Nijmegen-Cleve road.

The Calgary Highlanders split their force, sending one company to take Wyler from the rear and one east. This last made contact with 15th Scottish Division's left wing near Kranenburg by midday thus completing one of 2nd Canadian Division's tasks. But the capture of Wyler, essential for the opening of the main road, was much more difficult. The company sent to seize the town ran into stiff resistance from the Germans there who had had time to recover from the paralysing effect of the barrage and showed no inclination to surrender. After the Canadian company commander and

the commander of the leading platoon had both been killed a second company had to be committed and another bout of concentrated artillery fire brought down before the attack succeeded. Wyler was finally reported clear by 6.30pm but it took another two and a half hours before the roads were cleared of mines and traffic was able to move. This was some five hours behind schedule, a delay in opening the main road that was to have important effects on the fighting for Cleve.

By midnight 2nd Canadian Infantry Division had been squeezed out of the battle by the advance of 3rd Canadian on their left and 15th Scottish on their right. The Calgary Highlanders had 70 casualties of which 15 were killed and Le Régiment de Maisonneuve lost 22 of which only 2 were killed. The rest of 2nd Canadian's battalions who had been holding the front line were now gathered in but the division was not engaged again for another six days.

The 15th Scottish Division's task had the merit of brevity and clarity – 'to break the Siegfried Line and take Cleve'. To accomplish this, the main object of the first phase of the battle, they had been given very substantial support; the whole of the 6th Guards Tank Brigade – 178 Churchill tanks; two of 79th Armoured Division's regiments and two extra squadrons of flame-throwing Crocodiles and the 2nd Household Cavalry regiment. As well as first call on the heavy field guns and their own divisional artillery they had three regiments of mobile artillery, two batteries of self-propelled anti-tank guns and an anti-tank regiment.

Lying in front of this great force was a single regiment of German infantry with another behind deployed between Kranenburg and Cleve. The Germans had had, however, plenty of time to prepare their defences which consisted of a forward minefield, two lines of trenches covered by wire and mutually supporting

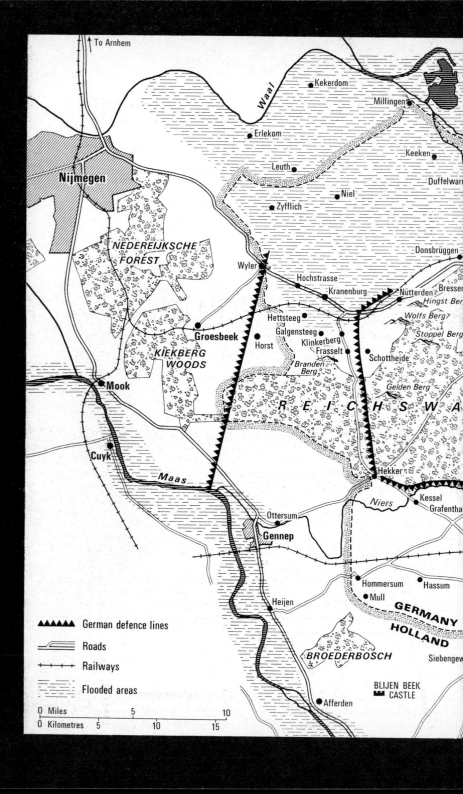

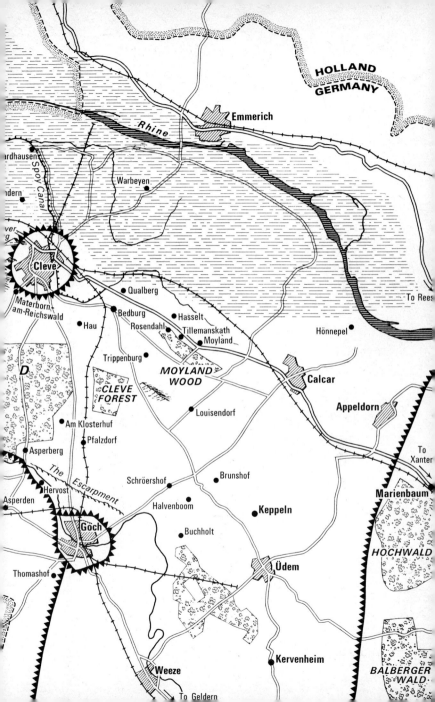

Machine gun crew of the Middlesex regiment operate amid growing mounds of used ammunition belts

machine-gun positions, and a wide anti-tank ditch beyond which were dug-outs, pill boxes and reinforced houses covered by mortar batteries, mobile guns and anti-aircraft batteries.

Major-General Barber decided to attack with two Highland Brigade groups moving side by side, as soon as there was room to do so, as far as the line Kranenburg-Frasselt. This was due to be secured by 4.0pm when the Lowland Brigade group would pass through them and, starting at 9.0pm breach the Siegfried defences in a night attack and capture Nutterden by 1.0am on 9th February.

Because of the narrowness of the assault front and the few roads only a fraction of 15th Scottish Division's massive strength could be used for the initial attack. On the right the 46th Highland Infantry Brigade sent in the Glasgow Highlanders supported by the tanks of the Coldstream Guards. With the assistance of the Flails of the

22nd Dragoons they were to advance 2,000 yards through a minefield and capture the villages of Haus Kreuzfuhrt and Hettsteeg. On the division's left the 227th Highland Infantry Brigade's attack consisted of the Churchills of the Scots Guards supporting the 2nd Argyll and Sutherland Highlanders. The tanks carried the infantry up to the start line through an old American minefield laid by the 82nd Airborne Division the previous September. The infantry then dismounted and together with the tanks started their attack into the forest. Their first day objective was the line from Klinkerberg, which is the northern extension of Frasselt, north to the wedge formed by the road and the railway running from Kranenburg to Cleve.

On 46th Brigade's right, twenty minutes before H-hour, the Glasgow Highlanders moved eastward out of Groesbeek together with a squadron of Coldstream Churchills. In front of them two troops of Flails had moved into the reported minefield, where all but one bogged down. This one beat a path through which all the Churchills followed in line. No mines were exploded and it was later discovered that none had been laid. The infantry kept up close to their own barrage and very little defensive fire was received. About noon, during one of the pre-arranged pauses in the artillery fire, the reserve companies leapfrogged forward, crossed the German frontier about 1.0pm and seized the two villages which were their objectives soon afterwards. The Glasgow Highlanders rounded up 230 prisoners and reported very few casualties themselves. The Coldstream lost several tanks in the deep mud but knocked out three anti-tank guns.

From behind, the next infantry battalion, the 9th Cameronians, came up right on schedule and advanced two companies up as soon as the barrage lifted at 2.15pm. By 3.0pm they had reached the Galgensteeg spur, which faces north a half a mile or so east of Hettsteeg. Here the elaborate field defences, well-wired and mutually supporting, could have given them a great deal of trouble but they had been abandoned in the face of the tremendous artillery fire. But in front of these defences there was an anti-personnel minefield into which the Cameronians' left-hand company advanced. Many men had their legs blown off and had to wait in the rain and the mud until stretcherbearers could be got up to them.

The 15th Scottish Division's right wing was on schedule and going well and the last phase of the first day's attack seemed ready to go in at 4.0pm as planned. This was an advance by the Cameronians' reserve company, supported by Churchills of the Coldstream and Crocodile flamethrowers, from the Galgensteeg spur down into the valley to capture Fressalt. But when the time came there was no sign of the Churchills or the Crocodiles who were finding it almost impossible to keep going through the deep, viscous mud. However some got through by 5.0pm and the attack went

in a quarter of an hour later. Half way to Frasselt the Churchills ran into a minefield and one was disabled but was still able to fire its gun in support of the infantry. The Crocodiles got through and burnt the houses in Frasselt flushing the Germans from the cellars to which they had fled from Galgensteeg defences when the barrage came down.

Frasselt was captured by 5.45pm and by 6.30 the Cameronians had two companies moved on to hold the higher ground further east and were in contact on the right with the left wing of 53rd Welsh Division. They had captured a battery of 88mm guns and forty-eight prisoners and had killed a great many more. The tanks had captured a battery of 105mm guns and had incurred no casualties in men but had lost several tanks to the mud as well as one to a mine. All in all 15th Scottish Division's right attack had done all that was expected of it by nightfall on the first day.

But the left attack, by 227th Highland Brigade, did not fare so well. The Germans manning the defences on their front came out remarkably quickly when the attack began and within a few minutes every officer of the Argyll's left forward company had been hit. The company sergeant-major then took command, rallied the company and continued the advance. By 11.40am leading companies were moving across the frontier into Germany and, during a pause in the barrage, the reserve company, the Highland Light Infantry, passed through the company which had lost all its officers and the assault continued on a two-battalion front.

The other leading Argyll company kept so close to the creeping barrage that they were able to capture Elsenhof and eighty prisoners together with a battery of 88mm guns without a shot being fired at them. During the afternoon the last of the Scots Guards' Churchills bogged down – eight were now stuck in front of Kranenburg – but some were able to support the

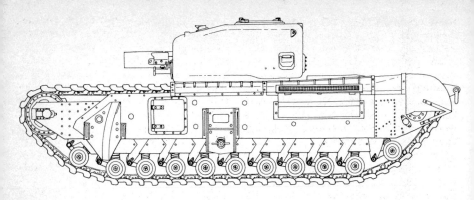

Based on the standard Churchill chassis, the AVRE (Armoured Vehicle Royal Engineers) was one of the special AFVs developed for the invasion of Europe by the Allies. It had been realised that the German defences would be based on well constructed concrete bunkers and pill-boxes, and that it was essential to neutralise these and allow a breach in the German defensive lines to be effected. For this the AVRE was produced. Its armament was a 25-pounder spigot mortar known as the Petard, and the projectiles from this proved capable of penetrating very substantial concrete walls. The vehicle was in constant demand as the Allies pushed forward into Germany and encountered progressively strong defence lines

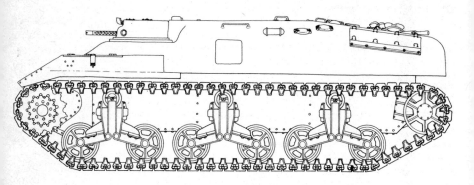

Typical of the improvised vehicles which were produced quickly when the need for them became apparent in the later stages of the war was the Kangaroo armoured troop carrier. It was produced by removing the turret from the Canadian-built Ram tank (which was designed to use British and American components already in production, but which never saw action as a tank). As a result of its improvised nature, the models produced varied considerably, depending on the workshop facilities available for the conversion. Most were able to carry ten infantrymen, and the usual armament was a single .5-inch machine gun

infantry with their fire and by 5pm Kranenburg had been captured together with some 300 prisoners.

The Highland Light Infantry advanced three companies up towards Kranenburg on the left of the Argylls and lost several men in a minefield because once again the Flail tanks were bogged. By afternoon, though, they had forced their way across the anti-tank ditch and then cleared the factory area to the south-east of Kranenburg and struck up to occupy the main road east of the town. By early evening they were in touch with the Canadian infantry on their left and the Argylls on their right.

By 6.30pm 15th Scottish left wing had carried out the first phase of their operation with complete success but some two hours behind schedule.

In the next sector south, on 15th Scottish Division's right, the 53rd Welsh Division advanced one brigade, the 71st, across an open valley against almost no opposition, across a natural anti-tank ditch and into the north-west angle of the forest. The infantry kept moving forward but practically all the vehicles except some of the Churchills bogged down. By 2.0pm the 1st Battalion Oxfordshire and Buckinghamshire Light Infantry had seized the important Branden Berg height. The plan then was to move the 160th Brigade up and through them to take the next heights, the Stoppelberg, but the only available road was badly congested and as the fresh infantry moved forward they came under heavy, accurate mortar and artillery fire. But one squadron of tanks managed to get through the boggy ground and across the ditch and with this support the infantry worked slowly but steadily during the night through the northern edge of the woods in soaking rain and reached the Siegfried defences shortly after midnight.

On the extreme right the 51st Highland Division had the hardest first day's fighting as they tried to clear a wide sector from a narrow base. Major-General Rennie decided to attack on the right with his 154th Infantry Brigade reinforced by the 5/7 Gordon Highlanders. The initial assault was made by the 1st Black Watch who took the first objective, the village of Breedeweg without difficulty but shortly afterwards German snipers killed three Black Watch officers. Tanks dealt with the snipers and the Gordons passed through but their vehicles were held up at the anti-tank ditch and only got to the edge of the forest as night was falling. They then became involved in heavy fighting with the battalion of the 1222nd Grenadier Regiment, which had been moved from 180th Infantry Division's sector the night before, and lost their momentum. Only when a battalion from the reserve brigade the 7th Argyll and Sutherland Highlanders, was committed was the advance continued and 148 prisoners taken.

The 152nd Infantry Brigade went through the breach opened by the 154th, the 5th Cameronians taking over from the 5/7 Gordons and pushing on into the forest stopping just short of Breedeweg village due to be captured by the 5th Seaforth Highlanders at first light the next day.

The 153rd Infantry Brigade first day's objectives were to form a firm base on the high ground in the south-west corner of the Reichswald, to push the Germans out of the thick woods nearby and to cut the Mook-Gennep road. The leading regiment were the 5th Black Watch but they were not able to move off until four o'clock in the afternoon because they had to use the same axis as the 154th Brigade. The 1st Gordon Highlanders followed the Black Watch an hour and a half later. Both battalions took their objectives in the forest without the help of tanks who got bogged down here as everywhere else along the front. But Flails cleared a lane through the first mine-field and an AVRE bridge carrier dropped its bridge across the anti-tank ditch enabling important supplies to be moved up to the forward troops – including 500 tins of self-heating soup.

Because of the stubborn German resistance 153rd Brigade's leading units were not firmly established in the southern corner of the forest until after midnight and it was not until 4.0am that the whole ridge which had been the Highland Division's objective was secured. Nor in this sector had the German defence collapsed as elsewhere along the front. They had withdrawn to prepared defences where they lay in considerable numbers ready for the continuation of the attack.

The battle did not stop during the night of 8th/9th February and there is no neat time to draw a line to mark the end of the first day's fighting. This was particularly true of the 15th Scottish and their supporting armour and of 3rd Canadian Division on the extreme left who had had to wait until 2nd Canadian had cleared Wyler and moved on before being able to launch their 'naval' operations in various amphibious vehicles. Both these divisions continued fighting all through the night.

In the case of 15th Scottish the plan called for the reserve brigade group, the 44th Lowland and the Grenadiers' tanks to move through the two Highland Brigades, cross the anti-tank ditch east of Frasselt, break through the Siegfried Line defences and seize the heavily defended area around Nutterden thus opening the northern axis, the main Nijmegen-Cleve road, through Nutterden. This attack was scheduled to begin at 9.0pm and Nutterden was to be clear by 1.0am. The original two brigade groups, having had time to refuel, draw ammunition, eat and rest, would then resume the attack which was intended to continue the northern axis into Cleve and to secure the high ground overlooking that town by daybreak. Even then there was to be no respite for the

Left: Floods test out the quality of American jeeps and half-tracks. The floods, caused by German demolition of dams, held up Ninth US Army for three weeks. *Above:* Scottish troops in action near Nijmegen

defenders of Cleve and the fourth stage of 15th Scottish Division's attack, to clear Cleve up to the line of the canal, was to take place at first light on 9th February. When this had been accomplished the reserve division, the 43rd Wessex, would be committed to exploit the breakthrough.

It was an ambitious plan but, considering the weight of infantry, armour and artillery available, not unreasonably so. What was not given due allowance though was the very bad state of the roads coupled with the steadily rising flood water. These things were to slow the Allies down much more effectively than the Germans.

By 6.30pm the two Highland Brigades who had made the initial assault had gained all their objectives but were two and a half hours behind schedule. It was the turn of the 44th Lowland Brigade who had been waiting all day at Nijmegen for their starting gun. It was planned that their Armoured Breaching Force, made up of Churchills of the Grenadier Guards, a section of flame-throwing Crocodiles, and a battery of self-propelled guns, would break a way through the German concrete defences for the infantry to follow. The Armoured Breaching Force had a squadron and a half of Crabs to flail paths through the minefields and a squadron of AVREs with SBG (small box girder) bridges or fascines for crossing anti-tank ditches. There were nearly 300 armoured vehicles in all and because of the flooded road the assault infantry were loaded into Kangaroos.

Two main axes had been assigned to 15th Scottish; the hard-surfaced road from Nijmegen to Cleve for 227th Highland Brigade and on their right a narrow, unmetalled track with deep ditches on either side for 46th Highland Brigade. But because of the stubborn German resistance in Wyler the main road could not be used and everything had to be funneled along the minor route – not only 46th Highland Brigade's attack force but all their supporting transport, the special tanks of 79th Armoured Division and five field regiments moving their guns up to cover the advance into Cleve.

The 44th Lowland Brigade's reconnaissance parties had been following the Highland Brigades all day and reporting back on the fast deteriorating route and at 9.0pm, by which hour the attack towards Nutterden should have been starting, when the order finally came for the reserve brigade to move out of Nijmegen, they knew the going was to be difficult. All night long the Armoured Breaching Force and the Kangaroos carrying the 6th King's Own Scottish Borderers who were to lead the assault struggled in the pouring rain along a track which had become a muddy nightmare.

The bridges on the AVREs were too wide and kept hitting the trees lining the track and snapping their supports which dropped the bridge into the lowered position. Any attempt to move off the road resulted in bogging so deep that some vehicles were never recovered.

After seven hours of this shambles in the rain and pitch dark, one company of KOSB, one squadron of Flails, two troops of AVREs with bridges and a mixed squadron of Grenadier Churchills somehow got to the anti-tank ditch. In the confusion none of the Armoured Breaching Force commanders could be found but the senior Grenadier Guards officer stepped into the breach. About 5.0am, some twenty minutes before first light, the attack was launched.

It was most untidy – there was no assembly area or forming-up place –

but on the command 'Advance' everyone just moved forward from wherever they were. The Flails advanced in five parallel columns through the minefield but it was the mud which proved the greater deterrent. Within half an hour three tracks had become so badly bogged they were quite useless. The few Flails still manoeuvrable, with engines roaring, struggled to beat two tracks to the anti-tank ditch. Quickly the AVREs followed and bridged the obstacle. As dawn was breaking the KOSB advanced across the bridge – only to have one of the towed anti-tank guns foul and block it completely.

The rest of the KOSB came back and, using the last path, got across a fascine-supported bridge. One company was now on the eastern side of the anti-tank ditch and immediately pushed forward and in a sharp attack seized the villages of Schottheide and Konigsheide together with a number of badly-shaken prisoners. The remaining three companies now came up and the important position was consolidated.

Half a mile ahead of the KOSB lay another section of the Reichswald through which a road ran straight to the Materborn feature but the entry into the woods was dominated from the north by a knoll about 150 feet high, the Wolfs Berg. It was now decided to bring up the Royal Scots Fusiliers through the KOSB to seize this high ground and continue the advance.

In the evening of 8th February the 2nd Gordon Highlanders (with their Scots Guards tanks) who, as 227th Highland Brigade's reserve, had not been used, were temporarily attached to 44th Brigade. They had advanced along the main road on the left, capturing a vital road bridge intact over the main anti-tank ditch, and advanced to Nutterden where they collected over two hundred prisoners from large concrete bunkers. By early morning of 9th February the situation on the Cleve front had been more or less restored and the attack was only a few hours behind schedule.

While the 15th Scottish had been struggling with collapsed communications all night long the 3rd Canadian Division had launched their attack across the flooded polder to clear the left flank.

The Germans had earlier blown the main dyke at Erlekom and the rising waters of the Waal had begun to flow through the hole in volume two days before the Allied attack. Drainage ditches collapsed under the shell-fire of the opening barrage so that this extra water was not carried off and during the first day's fighting the mile-long Quer Dam, just inside the German frontier, collapsed and soon the villages of Zyfflich and Niel, two of 3rd Division's early objectives, were completely surrounded by water.

The 3rd Canadian Division's commander, Major-General Spry advanced two brigades side by side, the 8th on the left who were ordered to seize the main dyke west of Zandpol and capture that place and the fortified village of Leuth a mile or so south, and the 7th on the right who were to 'sail' their Buffaloes in the dark north-east as far as the anti-tank ditch. This forward defence ran from a fortified customs house on the Alter Rhein south-east to Donsbruggen on the railway from Cleve to Nijmegen.

Radar-equipped Typhoons struck at the objectives, a heavy smoke screen was laid and at 6.30pm the attack

Prisoners of 53rd Division march away to the camps

started. On 8th Infantry Brigade's left two companies of the North Shore Regiment, carried in 79th Armoured's Buffaloes, quickly reached the main dyke and by 9.0pm were able to report Zandpol clear of Germans. On the Brigade's right Le Régiment de la Chaudiere, of French-Canadians, advanced on foot moving for much of the night through waist-deep, very cold water. This slowed them down but they captured their objective, Leuth, in a dawn assault on 9th February.

The 3rd Canadian Division's right attack by 7th Infantry Brigade was carried out by the Regina Rifle Regiment supported by tanks of the 13th/18th Royal Hussars. Here, as elsewhere on 3rd Division's front, very heavy smoke cover concealed the start of the attack and artificial moonlight – searchlights reflected off low cloud – lit the landscape ahead. The 'island' town of Zyfflich was captured in two hours and over one hundred Germans were flushed out of the cellars.

On the extreme right of 3rd Division's attack two companies of the Canadian Scottish 'sailed' in Buffaloes towards Niel, setting their course by compass. Either it or their navigation must have been faulty for they ran into a group of fortified houses about a mile south of their target and became engaged. The battalion's commanding officer, believing they were fighting for Niel, followed up with his command group. The Germans in Niel, alerted by the attack a mile south, were waiting and met the Buffaloes with withering fire from close range, wounding the CO and killing four others. At daybreak the missing companies, having overcome the earlier resistance and discovered where they were, came on and captured Niel.

By first light on 9th February 3rd

Canadian Infantry had captured all their first objectives and were continuing their sweep to clear the flooded Waal Flats completely. As 2nd Canadian Infantry had also completed their task, left flank protection was secured.

On the rest of the front everything had not gone precisely as planned and the capture of Cleve was some hours behind the time-table. This was particularly worrying for Horrocks had always been aware of the need to get into Cleve quickly – it had been the main reason for the stunning air and artillery attacks designed to eliminate resistance long enough for 15th Scottish Division's two Brigade Groups to smash into the town. Believing that the attack was going better than, in fact, it was, he sent a signal 'press forward' and put the reserve, the 43rd Wessex Division, on one hour's notice to move from midday on 9th February. At the same time the Guards Armoured Division, waiting at Tilburg, were warned to be ready to move from midnight of that day.

At dawn the following day, 10th February, Ninth US Army's supporting attack, Grenade, was due to be launched and when it came the Germans would find themselves without sufficient forces to hold either attacked front.

But it was essential that the momentum of the attack through the Reichswald be continued for the second day. The rain came down as though it would never stop; the water across the main Nijmegen-Cleve road rose eighteen inches in five hours; the unsurfaced tracks swallowed rubble from bombed houses, furniture, cars and knocked-out German vehicles but finally collapsed, the mud turned to black porridge. The appalling conditions gave the Germans the one thing they needed most desperately – time.

The Germans hit back

The Allied activity at the northern end of the long western front was watched carefully by the German High Command seeking to discover whether this was the long-awaited 'big blow' or a spoiling attack designed to draw them away from the bend in the Maas before the main assault came from south of Venlo. The farther away from the fighting the stronger was the opinion that the attack on the Reichswald was a subsidiary offensive.

German Intelligence at OKW West believed that the attack had been made with the 2nd and 3rd Canadian Infantry Divisions supported by a Canadian armoured brigade and consequently orders were sent to General Blaskowitz that no ground was to be given up and no reserves be committed yet.

At the other end of the command structure General Fiebig, whose 84th Infantry Division had had nearly six battalions destroyed by nightfall and General Straube, whose LXXXVI Corps had suffered over 3,000 casualties including 1,200 prisoners were both convinced that their front had been chosen for the Allies' main effort. The commander of First Parachute Army, General Schlemm, agreed with them and during the evening of 8th February was able to persuade the army group commander, General Blaskowitz to release the 7th Parachute Division for battle, but its units were widely spread and could only arrive piecemeal by battalions.

For the First Parachute Army it had been a terrible twenty-four hours beginning with air raids of a magnitude not experienced on their front before and followed by a five-hour artillery barrage greater than anything that had been seen on the western front in the Second World War. The barrage had continued with short pauses all through the day and the Allied Air Forces had pounded their rear areas, supply dumps, communications and headquarters with

A tank is left to its fate in the flooding

over 1,400 sorties all without the Luftwaffe putting in an appearance. Rocket-firing Typhoons had even attacked First Parachute Army's headquarters at Emmerich where among the killed had been the general commanding the army's artillery.

General Schlemm was pessimistic about the outcome; it seemed to him that having broken through the Siegfried Defences there was nothing to stop the British from sweeping on and capturing Cleve before he could bring up his reserve. The one place at which perhaps the Allies could be delayed was about a mile south-west of Cleve where two hills ran north and south near the village of Materborn am Reichswald. The westerly and lower ridge ran north-west of Materborn, the higher, easterly one through Bresserberg. Together they formed the 'Materborn Feature' which was so obvious a defensive position that the Allies had necessarily made its capture the first priority task after breaching the Siegfried Line, while on the German side it was the first place to be reinforced. It was a question of who got there first.

It will be remembered that the 15th Scottish Division's 44th Lowland Brigade had forced the anti-tank ditch and were established from Nutterden to Schottheide by early morning of the 9th. The 2nd Gordon Highlanders were on the left and the King's Own Scottish Borderers on the right and the original plan now called for a fresh regiment, the 6th Royal Scots Fusiliers to pass through the KOSB and seize the next two knolls, the Hingst Berg, east of Nutterden and the Wolfe Berg, about a half mile farther south. This would complete phase two of the 15th Scottish attack and, on the original schedule, was to have taken place by one o'clock in the morning on 9th February.

Because of the terrible road conditions there was no chance of the RSF getting up in time so the KOSB perforce had to continue the attack.

Two companies in Kangaroos pushed forward and by 11.15am had seized the Wolfe Berg with 240 prisoners and a medium battery. A little later the RSF got through along the main road, passed through the Gordons in the southern outskirts of Nutterden and captured the Hingst Berg. This was just after noon, some eleven hours behind schedule, and it was essential that no further time be lost in gaining the Materborn Feature.

At this point the original plan had called for the two Highland Brigades, rested and refreshed, to take over the lead again and, passing through the 44th Lowland Brigade, to capture the Materborn ridges and to sweep on into Cleve. But once again the almost impassable state of the few roads and the jam of vehicles made it impossible for two brigades to move through a third and it was necessary for the 44th Lowland to continue the fight. They had already been some thirty hours without sleep and fifteen on the move but in the early afternoon the Royal Scots Fusiliers and a squadron of Churchills of the Grenadiers from the 6th Guards Tank Brigade moved off against the westerly ridge north-west of Materborn. At about the same time the King's Own Scottish Borderers, supported by another tank squadron of the Grenadiers, drove east along forest tracks as fast as possible to seize the higher ground at Bresserberg, a half mile or so north-east of the RSF's objective.

The KOSB, on the left, were carried forward over the flooded track in Kangaroos of the 1st Canadian Armoured Personnel Carrier Regiment as far as the westerly slope of the Bresserberg Feature. The time thus saved was critical for they had no sooner seized the high ground and the village together with 160 prisoners and a battery of medium guns than they were in turn attacked by some of the German 7th Parachute Division, first of the reserves to make contact, who had been ordered to recapture Bresserberg. Although the KOSB succeeded in beating them off the Germans strongly reinforced the eastern slope of the ridge during the night and built defences out of the rubble and wrecked buildings of Cleve's south-western suburbs.

On the KOSB's right, the Royal Scots Fusiliers, together with another squadron of Grenadier's Churchills, advanced to the lower of the two ridges north-west of the village of Materborn. Here reports said there was a formidable defence system but once again intelligence was found to be faulty for the trenches were recently-dug and shallow and the Germans manning them seemed vastly relieved that 'for them the war was over'. Most remained quietly where they were and over seventy were captured. This was at 3.30pm but not long after, as the RSF were consolidating, they came under machine-gun and sniper fire from the 7th Parachute troops preparing their blocking position east of Bresserberg, about half a mile away.

Nevertheless by nightfall both ridges were firmly held by the tired but triumphant troops of the 44th Lowland Brigade and their supporting Guards Tank squadrons. With pardonable pride 15th Scottish Division reported that they had 'seized the Materborn Feature'. They believed that they had done so, greatly underrating the strength of the resistance the Germans were frenziedly throwing up around Cleve. The situation was most confusing for both sides because of the patchiness of the defence. The 15th Scottish Reconnaissance regiment, probing ahead, reported that the Germans in Cleve seemed to be still stunned and disorganised from the bombing and unlikely to offer resistance. General Horrocks received these optimistic reports at his command post and when, a little later, a further report that the 15th Scottish were 'moving into the outskirts of Cleve' was received he immediately unleashed the 43rd Wessex Division waiting in Nijmegen.

The plan, once the breach had been made, was to push a fresh infantry division with supporting armour through and, on the principle of Liddell Hart's 'expanding torrent', burst out into the plain east of Cleve. As we have seen the Siegfried defences were scheduled to be breached and Cleve captured some eleven hours earlier. Communications were not working well and just how bad the roads were was not known at corps' HQ so that when the news for which he had been waiting all day reached Horrocks he had no reason to doubt that the 15th Scottish were about to capture Cleve or that 43rd Wessex would have any difficulty in moving quickly up to them. But the route they were assigned, the main Nijmegen to Cleve road was under rising water and jammed with all kinds of vehicles from Nijmegen to Nutterden and it would be quite impossible for even the leading battalion, let alone an entire brigade group, to get up to the fighting at anything faster than a crawl.

In his memoirs General Sir Brian Horrocks says with characteristic frankness that his decision was one of the worst mistakes that he made in the war and he has certainly been criticised for committing his reserve too soon. Military historians in possession of the full facts and with ample time for consideration must beware of the temptation to be wise after the event. In the Battle of the Reichswald speed was the essence of the offensive and it was absolutely vital for Horrocks to debouch into the open country between Cleve and Goch and seize those places before the Germans could intervene effectively with their reserves. It had been confidently expected that the overwhelming superiority on the ground together with the tremendous barrage and concentrated bombing would ensure a rapid initial advance and the capture of Cleve within twenty-four hours. Therefore when, eight hours late, word came that the 15th Scottish were

moving into the city he had no reason to doubt it. He had not been fully informed of the really appalling road conditions and he says today (in an interview, November 1969) that he committed the first of his reserve divisions at the first opportunity because he was afraid of losing momentum. As the hours of the second day ran out it could be seen that the offensive was slipping behind schedule and the nightmare that loomed ahead was that XXX Corps' tightly crammed divisions might meet a counterattack from the main German strength while still in the bottle-neck. Without room to deploy and with the waters on either flank steadily rising the great offensive might be halted long enough for the Germans to create a defensive line based on the curve of high ground that runs from Calcar to Üdem which would link with the main Siegfried Line defences running south from Goch. Behind this line there would still lie another – the easternmost West Wall between Rees and Geldern. The main Allied objective, a speedy advance to the Rhine, would then have been missed.

In fact, although the sending of 43rd Wessex Division along 15th Scottish Division's axis produced one of the classic communications snarl-ups of the war, the end result, as we shall see probably justified it. Also, though Horrocks nowhere mentions the fact, it is interesting to speculate whether he would have thrown in the 43rd so quickly had he not been in the middle of a four-day attack of fever. (Interview, November 1969.) A temperature of 103 can increase a natural optimism wonderfully. Oftener than one might expect such small things determine the course of battles.

While 15th Scottish Division had been struggling hard to push the main thrust forward the other three divisions in the battle had been getting on with their tasks for the second day. They too were slowed by the flooding, the mud and, to give

97

credit where credit is due, by a recovery on the German side and stiffening resistance.

After capturing the Stoppelberg Feature, the 53rd Division's 160th Brigade pushed on to the north-eastern edge of the Reichswald and the 158th Brigade followed up from south of Frasselt to come up on their right. This was only some 1,000 yards from the German defence in front of Materborn. Also the second of the German reserve divisions, the 6th Parachute – which had been moved down from Arnhem, now began coming in south of Materborn. These troops attacked the 4th Welsh Regiment several times and although they were beaten off and lost six guns it was apparent that there would be no rapid advance across the important Cleve-Hekkens road.

The 53rd Welsh Division also suffered from the complete collapse of the roads in their rear which had to be closed for most of the second day while the engineers, reinforced with large working parties, used all their skill and ingenuity to make some sort of hard surface.

On corps' extreme right the 51st Highland Division attacked with the 5th Black Watch and the 1st Gordon Highlanders clearing the German anchor position in the Kiekberg woods and striking south to cut the Mook-Gennep road in two places. The Germans, mostly from 2nd Parachute Regiment, resisted spiritedly here and it was necessary to lay down a heavy artillery barrage and get the tanks up before the valley south of the woods could be cleared.

The Gordon Highlanders made a moonlight attack to clear a strong point only a mile and a half from Gennep. It was led personally by the Gordon's commanding officer who, after his troops had broken through the German position, was worried about coming unexpectedly on other Allied soldiers in the dark. He ordered

General Lüttwitz

his pipers to play the regimental march (thus cruelly adding to the discomfort of the Germans) and was delighted to hear faint answering strains of the pipes of the Camerons of Canada, (The Queen's Own Cameron Highlanders of Canada), who were attached to 51st Division for the battle.

At the same time as 51st Division's 153rd Highland Brigade were clearing the right the 152nd Highland Brigade took over the lead on the left. The 5th Seaforth Highlanders started their advance at dawn on 9th February and in mid-afternoon ran head on into a German counter-attack. By vigorous use of the bayonet they routed this attack and pushed on to the Kranenburg-Frasselt-Hekkens road where, about midnight, they were stopped by well dug-in German defences. On the 5th Seaforth's right the 2nd Seaforth also advanced in the dark until they were held up by a German strong point. Flame-throwing Crocodiles and AVRE Petards were requested to come up to assist in carrying the second line Siegfried defences at dawn the next day, 10th February.

On XXX Corps' left flank the second day had gone well too. Here the 3rd Canadian Infantry Division sailed in their amphibious vehicles into deeper waters. On the division's left the 8th Brigade captured Kekerdom and Millingen, westernmost German town on the Rhine: in the centre 7th Brigade advanced from Niel north to seize Keeken and the Custom House on the Alter Rhein which marked the northern end of the Siegfried Line defences. On 7th Brigade's right the village of Mehr was taken and with this most of 3rd Canadian Division's task had been accomplished, for the left flank was now secure along the southern bank of the Waal as far as a line drawn south from where the Alter Rhein flows in down to the main Cleve road east of Nutterden. The last objective to complete the Canadians' role in the opening phase of Veritable was to advance eastwards across the flooded flats as far as the Spoy Canal which connects the Alter Rhein with Cleve. That would be the task of the 9th Brigade, who were due to attack on 10th February.

Thus, by the end of the second day, all objectives of Phase One of the battle had been taken and the Germans had been roughly handled: 2,700 of them were prisoners of war and the 84th Infantry had lost eight battalions. Tasks for Phase Two were: on the right 51st Highland Division was to capture Gennep and Hekkens and clear the area in between in preparation for the attack on Goch; the 53rd Welsh Division were to clear the Reichswald Forest of all German troops as far as the Cleve-Goch road; the 43rd Wessex, passing through the 15th Scottish, were to wheel right and capture Goch, Üdem and Weeze; the 15th Scottish were to clear Cleve and push mobile columns towards Emmerich and Calcar. Also on 10th February Ninth US Army's great attack, Grenade, was due to go in on First Canadian Army's right and, by driving hard north-east, prevent the Germans from moving any reserves against XXX Corps' attack.

The First Canadian Army's Intelligence Summary forecast the probable German reactions thus: 'If he has forces available either from the Hochwald [a smaller forest east of Cleve] or from across the Rhine [i.e. in Twenty-fifth Army's sector] he will be tempted to try to regain Cleve or at least to seal it off. If he cannot do so then he must hold Goch and also cover the nearest Rhine crossings.'

This was more or less the German thinking on the third day of the battle except that they played one of their trump cards – the Roer dams. It will be remembered that Bradley's First Army had launched an attack against the dams on 5th February which had run out of steam after three days and that a fresh division, the 9th Infantry, had then been ordered to make an all-out attempt to gain possession of the dams by 9th February so that Grenade could start the following day.

The 9th Infantry launched their attack at first light but the Germans, well aware of the importance of the dams, defended every yard of the way. Meanwhile the water continued to rise on General Simpson's Ninth Army front because of the continual rain and it seemed to him that even if First Army captured the dams, as he was expecting every hour to hear, it would be reckless to send his army into an area in which the flood water was steadily deepening. Yet he knew that Veritable was already behind schedule and that Horrocks was depending very much on the let-up in pressure that Grenade would bring – it was a very difficult decision for one of America's most aggressive army commanders.

He told his corps commanders that he would decide by four o'clock in the afternoon of 9th February, the last possible moment if all the interlinking movements of a great attack were to begin. At four o'clock, reluctantly but with Montgomery's approval, he decided to postpone Grenade for twenty-four hours.

As the US 9th Infantry, supported by the 78th Infantry and a combat command of the 7th Armoured, forced their way towards the Schammenauel Dam the Germans fell back, maintaining a well-disciplined and hard-hitting rearguard. They had already decided what to do when it became obvious that they could hold the dam no longer; with Hitler's approval they blew the inlet gate to the tunnel and with other carefully calculated explosions jammed open the outlet gate. This meant that the hundred million tons of water poured out at a rate which would raise the floods opposite 9th Army and maintain them for the longest possible time.

The carefully calculated destruction took place during the night of 9th/10th February and by the next morning the Roer had risen five feet and was flowing too quickly for pontoon bridging. Montgomery visited Ninth

Army's front on 10th February and saw that Grenade would now have to be postponed for at least eleven days. This meant that the Germans would be free to concentrate all their available reserves against the First Canadian Army's attack. It was a hard blow and put paid to Horrocks' hopes of a quick advance to the Rhine.

When Eisenhower was approached he readily agreed to move two American infantry divisions to the British sector in order to release two British divisions to join the Battle for the Reichswald. These were the 52nd Lowland, another territorial division, and the 11th Armoured.

On the German side there was no longer any doubt of the strategic importance of the Allied attack

The devastation that followed German demolition of the sluices in the Schammenauel Dam over the Roer river

between the Waal and the Maas and Field-Marshal Gerd von Rundstedt the Commander-in-Chief West sent a signal to General Blaskowitz which said that the consequences of a break-through to the Rhine were 'incalculable' and that Cleve must be held 'at all costs'. Nor was there any longer any hesitation about committing reserves – XLVII Panzer Corps was ordered to move up to the battle and its commander, General von Lüttwitz, was put in overall control. His first target would be to secure Cleve, recapturing it if it should have fallen before his two panzer divisions could arrive. He would have, as extra infantry support, a regiment of the 346th Infantry Division from across the Rhine. Also, as we have seen, the 6th Parachute Division was being brought in on the German right.

It is probable that the comparatively slow reaction of the

M-10 tank destroyer in the Huertgen Forest

Germans to First Canadian Army's offensive was due to Führer HQ's preoccupation with the great Russian hammer blows on the Eastern Front and, more specifically, to the violent quarrels at this time (from 9th February to 13th) between Hitler and his Chief of the General Staff, Guderian, about Himmler's inept handling of affairs as the new Commander-in-Chief. Certainly direction from the top in Germany at this stage of the war showed none of the brilliance and professionalism of earlier periods. On the other hand it must be realised that after the failure of the Ardennes Offensive the Sixth SS Panzer Army had been moved to the east and the Germans in the west were hopelessly inferior in men and matériel – all Lüttwitz's two panzer divisions could put in the field were fifty tanks.

Meanwhile the rain continued to fall, the floods to rise, the mud to deepen, the routes to collapse and vehicles to move more and more slowly. Ammunition and fuel began to run low and fresh troops were unable to move up and through tiring ones. The battle, which was to have been an Allied blitzkrieg, was developing into what Eisenhower was later to describe to the Combined Chiefs of Staff, as a 'bitter slugging match in which the enemy had to be forced back yard by yard'.

But at the time only the comparatively few soldiers in the front line realised how difficult their task had become. Far away in Yalta Winston Churchill announced to Stalin and Roosevelt and their assembled aides that 'British troops began an attack at dawn yesterday in the Nijmegen area. They advanced about three thousand yards and are now in contact with the Siegfried Line. Tomorrow the American Ninth Army comes in and the British second wave will follow. The offensive will continue without cessation.'

A critical day

In the original plan the third day of Veritable was to have seen the capture of both Cleve and Goch and the establishment of a new start line through which the reserve divisions would pass and 'burst out into the plain.' Cleve was to be seized by 15th Scottish Division and 43rd Wessex in reserve south of Nijmegen, would then move through southern Cleve and wheel right for the attack on Goch.

Goch would also be attacked by the 53rd Welsh who, having come through the Reichswald, would wheel right as well. At the same time the 51st Highland Division on corps' right were to strike for Goch between the forest and the Maas. Left flank protection was the responsibility of 3rd Canadian Division whose objective was the line of the Spoy Canal.

Attacking through the Reichswald on a two brigade front the 53rd Welsh Division captured the two heights which dominated the forest. On the left the 160th Brigade's 4th Welsh Regiment captured the approaches to the Stoppel Berg during the morning and the 2nd Monmouthshire Regiment then went on to take the heights. On the right 158 Brigade's 1/5 Welch Regiment with tanks from 147 RAC captured the high ground west and north of the Gelden Berg Feature.

53rd Welsh Division had achieved their initial objectives by the end of the second day but communications were so bad that the main divisional axis had to be closed to all but traffic of the highest priority and every available man put to work to try to create a surface. 10th February was spent in patrolling and regrouping to establish a line along the Cleve-Hekkens road. On the same day the other divisions had their hands more than full.

The 43rd Wessex and their supporting 8th Armoured Brigade were released from reserve late on 9th February. They were expected to bypass Cleve shortly after midnight and advance to Bedburg. General Thomas planned to advance one brigade group through the Materborn Feature and to follow closely with his TAC HQ and his second brigade group so as to be able, as soon as they had reached open ground, to mount a powerful two-pronged assault against the Goch fortifications.

The 43rd Wessex were one of the original fourteen territorial divisions formed on 1st April 1908 when the old Volunteer Force ceased to exist. Due to the unpredictable circumstances of the war they spent the years from 1939 to 1944 in training and exercising in England, not getting into action until three weeks after D-Day. Their training had probably been the hardest in the British Army for their commander, Major-General Thomas, was determined that when his men went into battle they would encounter no conditions worse than those they had been subjected to on exercises and would not be asked to do anything, except kill, that they had not practised many times. His men called him 'von Thoma' but he was both respected and liked.

The 43rd were said by many to be the most overexercised division in the army and it was predicted that when the test came they would be found to be stale, like an over-trained athlete. But by February 1945 when Horrocks chose them to exploit the breakout from the Reichswald these doubts had been swept away as one by one the ancient west country regiments had proved their mettle and added to their battle honours. Battalions of the Wiltshire Regiment, the Dorset, the Worcestershire, the Royal Hampshire, the Somersetshire Light Infantry, the Duke of Cornwall's Light Infantry and their supporting arms had been in almost continual action since Normandy and before its commitment on 10th February the division had incurred some 10,000 casualties.

The full-scale fighting which now developed for Cleve and Goch was carried on by Brigade Groups. This large tactical formation had been developed from the lessons of the successful German blitzkriegs in the early years of the war and of later experience. By 1945 the brigade group had become a devastatingly powerful mixture of all arms (except air which was allocated anew each time) with, almost always, the right proportion of each.

The make-up of a brigade group differed slightly from one division to another but it consisted basically of three battalions of infantry (about 2,700 men), a battalion of tanks (sixty to seventy), a regiment of field artillery, a battery of anti-tank guns, a troop of self-propelled light anti-aircraft guns, a machine-gun company with a heavy mortar platoon and a field company of engineers. With rocket-firing planes and fighter bombers on hand and the right to call on the big guns in the rear, a brigade group was a miniature army.

The 43rd Wessex Division's 129 Brigade Group moved off first with some of the infantry of the 4th Wiltshire Regiment riding on the tanks of the Nottinghamshire Yeomanry (Sherwood Rangers) leading and a long column of other tracked vehicles, specialised armour, self-propelled guns etc. strung out behind. It was bitterly cold and the gusting wind flung needles of icy rain against the soldiers huddled on the backs of tanks or in troop carriers. Much of the route was under water and bogged vehicles on either side gave warnings of the depth of the mud.

The column crawled in fits and starts and as the hours dragged by the half-frozen men roundly cursed anyone who brought them to a halt, were bitter about the base wallahs

Field-Marshal Montgomery, General Horrocks, and Major-General G I Thomas commanding 43rd Division in informal conference

whom they pictured as sleeping soundly in nice warm beds, and cheerfully predicted a complete disaster when they finally encountered the waiting Germans. Kranenburg was reached about midnight, an average speed of less than two miles an hour and 4th Wilts' commanding officer went ahead and found the HQ of the 44th Lowland Brigade where he learned that the 15th Scottish were not in Cleve. Their leading infantry were some two miles short and the main road was blocked. Their reconnaissance however had found a way through by a secondary road which ran from just beyond Nutterden south-east through the forest.

It was decided that 129 Brigade would try to get past Cleve by this route. A troop of 15th Scottish Reconnaissance Regiment led the way with 4th Wiltshire following in Kangaroos.

Somehow in the dark and the rain the turnoff was missed and the column continued along the main road to Cleve running into the German forward outposts. The sudden bursts of Spandau fire emptied the Kangaroos in a matter of seconds. Infantry supported by tanks soon cleared this road block and the advance was continued with the 4th Wilts leading the way on foot trying to find a south-easterly route. They were followed by the tanks who fired their high explosive shells into every house and this, plus the enormous craters of the blockbusters dropped two nights before made progress very slow. Dawn found the 43rd Wessex Division stretched like a great snake with its head at the western edge of canal-side woods south of Cleve and the body winding back through the south-west suburbs of the town to Nutterden, where TAC HQ were frozen in a colossal traffic jam. Behind them 214th Brigade Group were jammed up all the way to Kranenburg. The 43rd Division's third brigade group, 130th, were still in Nijmegen.

The main German defences west of Cleve were on the eastern slopes of the Materborn and Bresserberg Features. Here survivors of the unlucky 84th Infantry Division had been reinforced by the first arrivals from 7th Parachute and were concentrating on preventing the 15th Scottish Division from advancing east from the high ground they had just won. The Germans were startled to discover at dawn on 10th February that more infantry and tanks had somehow blossomed in their rear. Their position would have been untenable if new German reserves, from 6th Parachute Division in the Arnhem area, had not now come on the scene. This was the 16th Parachute Regiment consisting of men originally selected for air-crew duties but converted into infantry in the last two or three months. They had had a minimum of training in ground combat (nor had any of them parachuted) but they were of high calibre, well-equipped, young, fresh and full of fight. Together with a few self-propelled guns, some artillery support and mortar batteries they flung themselves against the 129th Brigade Group.

The 4th Wilts had already been halted at the edge of the woods where the roads from Bedburg and Goch cross and now 4th Somerset Light Infantry were brought up on the left and 5th Wiltshire on the right and the position made into an all-round defence. The fighting raged all day among the ruins and bomb-craters and on more than one occasion it looked as though isolated groups of 43rd Wessex would be wiped out or their positions overrun but somehow it didn't happen and nightfall found the 129th Brigade Group still in place and more or less in control. They could not, however, continue their advance and were pinned down until new forces could be brought up.

Major-General Thomas whose TAC HQ had been stuck in the colossal traffic jam at Nutterden for hours and who had contracted a chill which was to lay him low for several days, had been trying to get his second brigade group, the 214th forward all day. There was a road of sorts leading south towards Materborn, reported by the Dutch Resistance to be of concrete, and he decided to send 214th Brigade down it. The divisional reconnaissance regiment was ordered to lead followed by the Duke of Cornwall's Light Infantry but, unfortunately, the reconnaissance were at the tail of 214th Brigade's long column. How they managed to push through the tanks, vehicles, towed guns and other transport of both the Scottish 227th Brigade and their own 214th Brigade is a mystery – it was one of the many 'impossible' feats of the battle.

They led the way down the track which turned out to be white sand and not concrete but they persisted and eventually emerged into the open ground east of the forest where they were immediately fired upon by some of the German defenders around Materborn. Their knocked-out vehicles and others which had bogged when trying to get away made it very difficult for the DCLI, who had broken out of the traffic jam in Nutterden and followed the reconnaissance, to get up and deal with the opposition. They did so by late afternoon and stormed the small village ahead at dusk eliminating the Germans there. However all attempts to continue the advance in the dark through Materborn to join up with 129th Brigade Group failed and it was finally decided to wait until dawn.

Meanwhile the steadily rising floodwater had made the main road impassable to all but special vehicles or three-ton lorries and 43rd's reserve, the 130th Brigade Group, could not move up from Nijmegen.

The 43rd Wessex Division should have been well clear of Cleve by nightfall on 10th February but the colossal traffic jams, the cratering and German resistance had prevented this. The fact that 129th Brigade Group were pinned down in the south-western suburbs of Cleve made 15th

Scottish Division's task for 10th February impossible. It had been intended to leave 44th Lowland Brigade holding the Materborn Feature and for 227th Highland Brigade to advance from Nutterden and clear Cleve. Meanwhile 46th Highland Brigade were to get a mixed column of tanks, infantry and self-propelled guns ready to pass through 227th and exploit beyond Cleve as far as Calcar. A second mobile column would strike north from Cleve towards Emmerich.

The first snag to this plan came when 227th's commander tried to send the Argylls and the Gordons (now returned to his command) on Scots Guards tanks through 43rd Wessex Division towards Donsbrüggen and a hill about a mile south of it. To facilitate this move the 43rd had been ordered to move their second Brigade Group, the 214th, off the road for two hours from 8.0am. It was easier ordered than carried out, for the congestion had been getting worse as minor roads collapsed and units were shunted on to the main one and all sorts of rear units tried hard to get up – the huge guns of 15th Scottish artillery to support the attack on Cleve, the special vehicles of the 79th Armoured Division, signals, ambulances, ammunition trucks and other supply vehicles. The 214th Brigade could not get off the road for the side lanes were jammed and the ground between covered with bogged down vehicles.

Most commanders believed that they had priority and were not disposed to yield their ground. Frustration begat anger and the language that was heard was not fit for genteel ears – fortunately there were none. As the historian of the 43rd Wessex Division (who was in command of 214 Brigade) put it with soldierly understatement: 'In the circumstances it is not surprising that throughout the day the contacts of many of the commanders involved had been of a character which cannot

justly be described as being note-worthy for their cordiality.'

On the left the Royal Scots Fusiliers drove east along the main road for Cleve and after some fierce and costly fighting established themselves on top of a hill, the Cleverberg, only about a mile and a half from the centre of the city. Some of the German troops which had been holding in this area withdrew south-east which brought them into contact with 129 Brigade Group who assumed that this was a fresh counter-attack and called for an artillery bombardment on the Cleverberg Feature. Caught without cover all four of RSF companies suffered casualties from 43rd Division's guns.

It had been intended that the Royal Scots and the KOSB would advance on the right from the Materborn Feature into Cleve at the same time as the RSF made their attack but this was found to be impossible because the 129th Brigade Group were en-tangled with the Germans all through the south-western suburbs of Cleve which lay ahead of the Scots infantry making it quite impossible to lay down a creeping barrage. To try to advance into the machine-gun in-fested ruins without artillery support would have been throwing lives away.

The 44th Lowland Brigade's com-mander suggested, and his divisional commander agreed, that the only thing to be done was to wait for first light the next day and then for them to move forward and take over 129 Brigade's positions 'in an orderly manner'. Once 129 had been relieved and moved south, 44th Brigade could get on with their task of clearing south of Cleve. The 46th Highland Brigade were ordered up to take over the Materborn feature from 44th Lowland and 227th Highland were to concentrate at Donsbrüggen and launch an attack to clear Cleve from the north on 11th February.

But it had not been all disappointment and bad news on the 10th February: progress towards the main objective had been slow but the supporting attacks in the north, the centre of the forest and on the southern flank all gained ground although here too the quite unusually bad conditions prevented the original optimistic timetable from being maintained.

On the left the 3rd Canadian Division found that the floods prevented their supporting artillery moving up and their attack, by 9th Infantry Brigade, was delayed until 4.30pm. It was then launched without artillery support. The Stormont, Dundas and Glengarry Highlanders sailed their Buffaloes straight to Donsbrüggen where they linked with the 2nd Gordon Highlanders of 15th Scottish Division and then pushed on north-east to the next village, Rindern. Here they fought for some five hours from about midnight until dawn but were unable to push the Germans out and reach their objective, the Spoy Canal, less than a mile farther on. On the left of the SD&G advance the Highland Light Infantry of Canada also began their assault at 4.30pm but were stopped after a mile by German machine guns protected by pillboxes and completely covering the only approach. Here the Canadians spent the rest of the night and the Germans, survivors of 84th Infantry's 1052nd Grenadier Regiment, quietly fell back to Wardhausen on the western bank of the Spoy Canal – the Canadian's objective for 10th February. But as 15th Scottish had not yet captured Cleve the delay was of no great importance.

On the extreme right of Operation Veritable the 51st Highland Division met with mixed fortunes on the third day but continued their difficult task

of clearing the well-defended area between the southern edge of the Reichswald and the Maas. The 2nd Seaforth Highlanders, who had been held up by a particularly well-sited German strong point at dusk on 9th February, now called up the assistance of the specialist armour and their own tanks to break through on 10th February.

The strong point was part of the Siegfried Line defences and consisted of three large pillboxes constructed of four-inch steel and two-foot concrete and sited so as to be self-supporting and to give an all-round field of fire. The sleeping quarters were underground in the centre with interconnecting tunnels. The whole area was mined and covered by trip wires. The British method of dealing with this kind of position, designed so that a few determined men could hold up a great many, was known as 'The Drill'. It had evolved from experience and was most effective. First smoke was used to isolate one of the pillboxes and then high explosive shells were fired directly into the embrasures. An AVRE Petard then came forward and launched its 'dustbin' at the embrasure, blowing it in; this was followed by the flame-throwing Crocodiles. If necessary – and it seldom was – the remaining pillboxes were dealt with in the same way.

The strong point was eliminated and 152 Highland Brigade with its supporting tanks (from 34th Armoured Brigade) forced its way to the Kranenburg-Hekkens road. The intention now was to wheel right and capture the important road junction of Hekkens but the southern portion of the main anti-tank ditch ran just east of the road and it was manned by well-armed Germans determined to hold their positions. The 5th Seaforth Highlanders were pinned down in a ditch only fifty yards from the German positions and the 5th Cameron Highlanders, though wiping

Left: The disastrous flooding. *Above:*
Self-propelled 17 pounder on the
outskirts of Nutterden

out five machine-gun positions in a
series of bayonet charges, were also
held as was the third battalion in
152 Brigade, the 2nd Seaforth Highlanders. The 154th Highland Brigade
were then ordered to come up and
move through their positions and
capture Hekkens.

The 153rd Highland Brigade's task
for 10th February was to capture the
small but important township of
Gennep on the south bank of the
River Niers. The 5th Black Watch and
the 1st Gordon Highlanders attacked
south-east along the axis of the Mook-
Gennep road and reached the village
of Ottersum on the north bank of the
Niers river in daylight. At night both
battalions crossed the river in assault
boats and the Black Watch captured
Gennep.

By now the flood waters of the Roer,
fed by the blown Schwammenauel
outlet gate, had spilled over into the
Maas and its tributaries. The Niers,
usually less than 100 feet wide in
February had swollen to nearly 200.
From the high ground south of the
river the Germans could deny 51st
Highland Division the use of the main
road to Goch, their final objective. It
was now necessary to cross the Niers
in strength, capture Kessel and clear
this high ground; it was also absolutely imperative to gain possession
of the Hekkens crossroads, a key to
the communications south of the
Reichswald and an anchor position of
the Siegfried Line.

For the Allies the third day of their
offensive, the end of what is commonly
accepted as the critical period, had
been intensely frustrating, particularly at the *schwerpunkt*, the attack
against Cleve. This town was a key
position for the success of the whole
offensive as both commands knew and
had escaped capture because of the

flood and the mud and the communications paralysis brought about when two divisions tried to use the same axis at the same time.

It was now apparent to Crerar and Horrocks that this was to be no blitzkrieg, no surprise overwhelming of a weak defence and a twenty-mile advance to the Xantern-Geldern line. Maintenance of supply was going to be a major problem and with fresh German forces arriving it was going to be a hard slog in the mud against an enemy unexpectedly given a respite and, because of the protection of the Roer floods, allowed to commit all his reserves against them.

The breaks had gone against First Canadian Army but luck like weather is usually evenly distributed in the long run. As soon as the weather cleared, as it must, the tremendous power of the Allies' air forces could be brought into play; as soon as the floods abated, as they must, the American Ninth Army would launch Grenade and the Germans would have almost nothing to oppose them with.

But meanwhile it was important to maintain the momentum however difficult that would be with tiring troops and the dreadful conditions. There could be no change in the immediate objectives; Cleve must be captured so that exploitation to Calcar could take place; the Reichswald would have to be cleared completely so that communications could function; the Siegfried Line would have to be broken and the strongly-fortified town of Goch would have to be stormed to allow the offensive to expand through Weeze and Üdem.

Although the 15th Scottish, the 53rd Welsh and the 51st Highland Divisions and their supporting armoured brigades had been more or less continuously engaged for three days they would have to ignore fatigue, get their second wind and

Congestion in the lines of communication. Nijmegen in February 1945

carry the attack forward. The reserve, 43rd Wessex, with one brigade pinned down in the suburbs of Cleve, a second halted before Materborn village and a third unable to move out of Nijmegen, would have to break clear of its shackles and drive hard and fast southwards. Conditions made it impossible to use the waiting Guards

An Avre Churchill tank makes a turn on difficult ground near Cleve

Armoured Division and though more reserves were on the way they could not arrive at the battle for several days. A quick victory was no longer possible.

News of the failure of Montgomery's great blow at the northern end of the front to achieve a quick breakthrough was not entirely unwelcome to his rivals and Bradley telephoned Patton about it late on 10th February. 'Monty's alleged attack is the biggest

mistake Ike has made in this war!' he said. He went on to explain that it had bogged down completely and predicted that Grenade would be scrapped and the main Allied effort switched to the south, to Patton's front.

But neither Eisenhower or Montgomery had even thought of changing the overall strategy. They had blundered badly over the Roer dams for it should have been apparent that the Germans could always use the mass of water in the way they did and therefore the seizing of the dams should have had priority over both the mounting of Grenade and Veritable. However the damage had been done and it was going to be more difficult to drive the Germans back to the Rhine – more difficult but with the enormous superiority of arms and men, absolutely inevitable.

Advance
to contact

By the third day of the assault through the Reichswald the German High Command at last realised that this was indeed the opening of the Allies' great offensive. The main axis was obviously Kranenburg-Cleve-Calcar-Xanten, the key to the Rhineland, and Rundstedt decreed that Cleve must be held 'at all costs'. To this end he released his sole armoured reserve, XLVII Panzer Corps. Its commander was ordered to assemble at Üdem to take charge of the battle and to hold Cleve and the high ground south-west of it, recapturing both, if necessary.

The order committing the mobile reserve was given on 10th February and XLVII Corp's two divisions, the 116th Panzer and 15th Panzer Grenadier, arrived in the assembly area the following evening. By that time the situation had changed drastically.

At the northern end of the front the 3rd Canadian, 15th Scottish and 43rd Wessex all resumed their attacks on 11th February. The Canadians had little left to do to complete their task and the Highland Light Infantry of Canada, who had halted before Duffelward the night before, took the town without loss at dawn and advanced swiftly eastwards a mile or so to Wardhausen which they occupied, after mopping up German resistance, by early evening. They then moved up to the west bank of the Spoy Canal and started to deploy along it. On their right the Stormont, Dundas and Glengarry Highlanders, who had had a company fighting in Rindern all night, sent in two more at daybreak and cleared the town by mid-afternoon. They too pushed on to the Spoy Canal and joined up with the troops from Wardhausen. Before midnight on the 11th the 3rd Canadian Division were firm along the west bank of the canal from where it joins the Alter Rhein south to the outskirts of Cleve.

The 15th Scottish Division, determined to make up for lost time,

German tank in a snowstorm

launched a two-pronged attack against Cleve on 11th February with 227th Highland Brigade and the Scots Guards' tanks on the left and 44th Lowland Brigade and the Grenadier's tanks on the right.

But before this could take place 44th Lowland had to move forward and relieve the 43rd Division's 129th Brigade whose troops had been engaged during all the night. While 15th Scottish infantry were moving forward here the Germans launched a fierce, determined attack against the 5th Wiltshire. After an hour's heavy fighting they were beaten off and the British infantry counter-attacked the German positions and took 180 prisoners. Soon afterwards the King's Own Scottish Borderers and the Royal Scots arrived and by 10.30am the near-exhausted troops of 129 Brigade were able to stand down, to get a hot meal and then to sleep among the ruins of Cleve, their first real sleep for over fifty hours.

The 44th Lowland Brigade continued to clear the southern suburbs of Cleve advancing north-east towards the centre of the town. Their reconnaissance had drawn fire from the high ground to the north at first light but the Royal Scots Fusiliers, with the help of the Grenadier's Churchills dealt with this opposition. Slowly but steadily the Scots moved into Cleve.

On 44th's left the Argyll and Sutherland Highlanders of 227 Brigade were relieved by the 46th Highland Brigade from their positions atop the Materborn Feature who then advanced towards Cleve along the main road from Donsbrüggen. The Gordon Highlander's and the Scots Guards' tanks led the way reaching the crossroads at the eastern edge of the woods at dusk having encountered nothing more serious than bazooka fire from the wooded slopes which was quickly and efficiently silenced by the infantry.

In the failing light the leading troops of 15th Scottish Division's converging attacks mistook each other for the enemy and opened fire but fortunately this new war between Highlanders and Lowlanders was stopped before there were many casualties.

Cleve was almost unrecognizable as a city; the roads practically impassable because of yawning bomb craters or collapsed houses and no living thing to be seen. Only some of the cellars which had been reinforced and turned into last-minute defence positions, were found to be still intact. But – and this was even more welcome than shelter from the rain and cold – they were found to be stuffed with food: smoked sides of ham, dried fish, sausages, cheeses, black bread and barrels of pickles. After four days of almost continuous fighting on compo rations the 15th Scottish infantry were ready for a change. They feasted themselves, regretting only the uncivilised lack of whisky.

Forward companies of the Gordons pushed through the ruins and cap-tured a damaged road bridge over the Spoy Canal just south of the blown railroad bridge. A small force scrambled across the girders and established a bridgehead while the sappers came up and repaired the bridge for road traffic. Just after 3.30 am the brigade reserve, the 10th Highland Light Infantry, with a squadron of Scots Guards' tanks and some 79th Armoured's Crocodiles in support, moved across the canal and cleared the north-east part of Cleve before dawn on 12th February.

The 15th Scottish Division's next move was to bring forward 46th Highland Brigade and their supporting armour, to advance quickly east and seize Calcar.

Meanwhile 43rd Wessex Division's second brigade, the 214th who, it will be remembered, had been held up before Materborn village at last light on 10th February, had vigorously continued their advance. During the night of 10th/11th February a company of the Duke of Cornwall's Light

The ruins of Cleve

Infantry probed forward behind the German line to search out the lie of the land. As a result of the information they brought back the brigade commander decided to overwhelm the defenders in Materborn village and to push his forces on quickly to seize the dominating high ground which runs from Bedburg-Hau east of the Cleve-Goch railway to the Reichswald. A set-piece attack was laid on for 11th February to overcome the resistance in Materborn village: first a tremendous pounding by the divisional artillery and then an infantry/tank attack by the DCLI and the 4th/7th Dragoon Guards.

This massive strength practically demolished the comparatively small German position. Most of the defenders fled leaving their equipment behind but, inevitably, there were a few who, despite the odds, chose to stand and fight and die and they held up 7th Somerset Light Infantry, the second assault wave. Finally the 'Sets' broke clear of Materborn village and

pressed on but about a half a mile east of the village they were met by a hail of Spandau fire coming from a key crossroads about a quarter of a mile farther on.

Supported by fire from the tanks the Somersets advanced and although one of the Churchills was knocked out by a self-propelled gun and the houses were crammed with German infantry the crossroads was cleared by 5.0pm on 11th February. But the light was going, heavy sleet was worsening the visibility and the objective, Hau, was still another half mile away.

As it was no use trying to advance the tanks through the dark they were pulled back into a tight laager for the night and the tired infantry set off through the sleet and blackness to push down the straight, unprotected road. Machine-gun and small arms fire belched from every house and the going was slow and costly. After five hours little ground had been cleared. It was midnight and the Somersets were reaching the end of their endurance. Their commander decided to send his leading company straight down the road ignoring any Germans who might be on either side leaving them to be dealt with by the following companies.

By two o'clock in the morning the near-exhausted infantry had advanced south along the Goch road to a bend south of Hau. On their right was the dark tree-line that marked the eastern edge of the Reichswald; ahead, to the left, lay the isolated small Forest of Cleve. Between the two ran the main communications between Goch and Cleve, both road and rail. Another company of the Somersets had gone into the village of Hau where hand-to-hand fighting went on all night.

The 1st Worcestershire Regiment had followed 7th Somerset from Materborn village and had moved through the crossroads and advanced another quarter of a mile east along the road to Bedburg-Hau. Here, at dawn, they came under heavy machine-gun fire but overwhelmed the Germans in the houses in a series of rushes and, on learning that the artillery barrage planned to support their next advance could not take place for three hours, advanced without artillery to the high ground west of Bedburg. Thus early morning of the 12th February found 214 Brigade's two battalions firm upon their objectives after many hours of close-quarter fighting in the dark. They were facing south-east along a two-mile line, from west of Bedburg to where the Reichswald comes up to the Cleve-Goch road. During the morning 7th Somersets, on the right, made contact with 53rd Welsh Division who had fought their way through the centre of the forest.

The 43rd Division's 129th Brigade had resumed their advance too, after a few hours' rest. The 4th Somerset Light Infantry had led, moving down to the minor road which runs east along the Spoy Canal south of Cleve. On the right of this road there were narrow woods; on the left the canal. The Germans had laid mines thickly between the two and the road was badly damaged by the enormous craters of the blockbusters. The mines and the cratering combined with small-arms fire and mortaring from high ground at the far end of the wood made the going very difficult. But the mines were lifted, the craters by-passed and the resistance on the ridge driven off and the 4th Somersets finally emerged from the bottleneck only to come under heavy fire from infantry dug-in along the railway embankment.

Mortar fire was brought down on these troops and they were then attacked by tanks and infantry. After a short, bloody spell of fighting the embankment positions were cleared, fifty prisoners taken and as many more German dead left for others to deal with. The reserve was now passed through and by nightfall had captured Bedburg and linked up with 214 Brigade.

The 43rd Wessex Division had at last shaken free of the rubble and jammed roads of Cleve and reached a position from which to launch the next, and final, part of their attack – the advance south to Goch. The immediate task was to seize the ridge south-east of Bedburg and, using it as a start line, advance another half mile or so to capture the village of Trippenburg through which ran the third Siegfried Line defences between Cleve and Goch. This ridge was scheduled to be captured on the next day, 13th February.

The 43rd Wessex Division's reserve brigade, the 130th, was still at Nijmegen, for now the water had risen to four feet on the section of road between Beek and Nutterden. It was therefore placed under command of the 53rd Welsh Division and ordered to move up along their axis through the Reichswald and take part in the attack on Goch. The 43rd's divisional

artillery were now emplaced on the Materborn Feature from where they fired day and night for the next three days supporting the desperate and costly attempts to break the Germans' new defence line.

In the forest itself the 53rd Welsh Division had resumed their advance on 11th February planning to put 160 Brigade on the left and 158 Brigade in centre and through the Reichswald to secure its eastern edge. First movement was from the eastern slopes of the Stoppel Berg when the 6th Royal Welch Fusiliers and the 2nd Monmouthshire Regiment advanced across the Materborn-Hekkens road. The RWF met little opposition but the Monmouthshire, after passing through the 4th Welch lines, came under heavy cross fire. Despite losing forty men they pushed on and captured their objective. The 4th Welch then leap-frogged through them and captured Dammershof along with prisoners and a self-propelled gun.

Farther south on 158 Brigade's front the 1st East Lancashire Regiment and the 1/5 Welch Regiment crossed the road, wheeled right and struck for the little village of Am Klosterhuf and the crossing over the Niers south of Asperberg.

It was difficult going with the German self-propelled guns firing straight down the long rides while being protected themselves by close-planted trees and absence of other approaches but despite casualties to both men and tanks the East Lancashires reached the Cleve-Asperden road by 6.30pm. But the 1/5 Welch on their left were held up a half mile short of the road and the 7th Royal Welch Fusiliers, coming up behind them, ran into trouble from troops

Panzerfaust grenadiers in action

which the leading battalion had apparently bypassed.

At 8.30pm orders came from Division that both brigades were to halt, consolidate and prepare plans for resuming the advance the next day, 12th February. Encouraged by this pause the 2nd Parachute Regiment launched a strong counter-attack to push the East Lancashires back into the forest and regain control of the Cleve-Asperden road but were beaten off.

While 15th Scottish and 43rd Wessex Divisions had been capturing Cleve and breaking clear of the shackles of its cratered streets and shattered ruins and 53rd Welsh Division had advanced to the eastern edge of the Reichswald, the 51st Highland Division, on XXX Corps' right, had been continuing their difficult task of clearing the ground between the forest and the Maas and breaking through the formidable Siegfried Line fortifications west of Goch.

It will be remembered that 152 Brigade's attack against Hekkens had been stopped in its tracks by the fire of the Germans manning the anti-tank ditch in front of that place and that 154 Brigade had been ordered to come up and move through 152 and capture Hekkens. It took most of 11th February for this move to be completed and there was some question of postponing the attack until dawn the next day for it was agreed that a night advance through the woods against a well dug-in enemy was not feasible. However, there was still about an hour and a half of light left so at 3.30pm two Black Watch battalions, the 1st and the 7th, moved off together from a start line a mile and a quarter from the village. Because it was so well-fortified and the forward defence line consisted of dug-in Spandau positions, maximum artillery support and the aid of flame-throwing tanks had been asked for. A troop of Crocodiles from 1st Fife & Forfar Yeomanry of 79th Armoured Division flamed the machine-gun positions and

almost the entire XXX Corps artillery fired their guns on the Hekkens position. As soon as the barrage began to roll forward the Black Watch moved off from their start line keeping so close behind the exploding shells that the stunned Germans had no time to recover before the Scots were upon them. By 7.0pm on 11th February the troublesome strong point had fallen and over 200 Germans had surrendered.

On the 10th of February 153 Brigade had captured Gennep with the 5th Black Watch but had found that many Germans had barricaded themselves in houses and were determined to hang on as long as possible. The 1st Gordon Highlanders came forward and set about clearing out these stubborn defenders by a method they had evolved in the street fighting in Holland. While mortar and machine-gun fire was directed against the front of a row of houses the infantry attacked each in turn through the back garden until an entire street had been cleared on one side. Then the opposite side was dealt with in the same way.

On 11th February two troops of Buffaloes of 79th Armoured started a ferry service over the Niers at Gennep which brought down heavy and accurate shelling and mortar fire. The loading area was changed and the ferrying continued without a break and a whole battalion of the 5/7 Gordons were moved over the river by 5.0pm. The ferrying operation then began to falter but this was due to mechanical difficulties as the overstrained engines and gear boxes of some of the amphibious tanks gave way. Maintenance work went on all night and a second battalion of the Gordons was ferried across the next morning, 12th February. By noon the engineers had succeeded in getting a bridge in and some of 1st Fife & Forfar's Crocodiles were able to get across to Gennep and burn out the last

The defenders cross a road under fire

of the Germans still bravely holding out.

After four days of the offensive, although well behind schedule and encountering stiffening resistance, XXX Corps' divisions had all reached positions from which the second phase of the battle could be mounted. In the north the 15th Scottish planned to advance from Cleve to Calcar while the 43rd Wessex wheeled right and struck for the high ground north of Goch. Nearing the forest's eastern edge the 53rd Welsh intended to put two brigades across the north to south roads and to mop up behind them with their third brigade. They would also make every effort to capture the bridge over the Niers at Asperberg. On the southern flank the 51st Highland Division now had to cross the flooded Niers in force and clear the area south of it in order to be able to mount an attack on Goch from the west.

Let us see how well these plans succeeded.

From Cleve, at 11.0am on 12th February a 'Jock' column moved out of the north-eastern suburbs and took the main road to the south-west. This was that part of Veritable's second phase which had originally been assigned to the Guards Armoured Division who were to erupt from Cleve in a one-day lightning strike through the disorganised Germans to Wesel and the Rhine. But the inland lake that now lay between Horrocks' reserve armoured division and Cleve prevented their moving up and 15th Scottish had to continue the assault. The task was given to 46th Highland Brigade Group and the force allotted consisted of the 7th Seaforth Highlanders, a squadron of Coldstream tanks, a squadron of 15th Scottish Reconnaissance, Kangaroos of the 49th Royal Tank Regiment and the Canadian Armoured Carrier Regiment, Crocodiles of the 141st Battalion Royal Armoured Corps, a battery of self-propelled guns and a platoon of engineers with their specialist equipment.

The assault, intended to move swiftly before the Germans could recover from the loss of Cleve, was delayed for over two hours when one of the Churchills hit a mine at a narrow, mud-surrounded section of the road less than a mile from the start line. The reconnaissance armoured cars waited just east of Cleve until a detour was cleared but it was not until 1.30pm that the Kangaroos and Churchills got up to them. The advance was then resumed but almost immediately ran into trouble.

At Qualberg, a small village two miles east of Cleve, bazooka and small arms fire was received. The Kangaroos dropped their infantry but were then ordered to take the lead – not surprisingly four of them were knocked out by a self-propelled gun whose crew had been patiently waiting for just such an opportunity. The knocked-out Kangaroos – two of them were blazing – completely blocked the road but while one Guards' tank towed them away another advanced and scored a direct hit on the side of the SP. At the same time the Seaforths stormed the well-defended houses, killing twenty-five Germans and capturing sixty-five for a loss of twenty-five of their own men. Qualberg was cleared by 3.0pm.

Now German shells and mortars were falling continuously but the column pushed on to the next village, Hasselt. Here they again came under heavy small arms and machine-gun fire from the houses and two more self-propelled guns opened fire. Once again the Seaforths began to clear the houses and the Coldstream to engage the 88s. The light was fading fast, the German shelling was very heavy and when a report (subsequently discovered to be untrue) was received that 43rd Wessex were being 'heavily counter-attacked by numerous infantry and tanks' at Bedburg, less than a mile to the right and behind them, the Seaforth's commander decided that it would be folly to leave so comparatively small a force in an exposed position all night. The brigade commander agreed and the column drew back to Qualberg. Here the infantry formed a tight defence and the armour continued all the way back to Cleve.

The decision to stop the drive for Calcar and to pull back two miles from Hasselt to Qualberg at dusk on 12th February was a prudent one, for new German forces, including panzer divisions, had been identified and an unknown number of 88s had opened fire. Nor was there any reason to doubt the reports of a large German mixed force attacking the brigade groups on their right. Undoubtedly the 7th Seaforth Highlanders and their supporting tanks and self-propelled guns in Hasselt were in an exposed position, but with the Germans badly off balance and desperately trying to create a stop line it was a time for taking risks rather than for prudence. It certainly was not the time to lose hard-won momentum.

The strength at 46th Highland Brigade's point was not inconsiderable: about 300 infantry, fourteen tanks and a battery of self-propelled anti-tank guns. Immediately behind were some 500 more infantry and another twenty tanks while in Cleve, which was handed over to the 7th Canadian Brigade on the 12th, there were another 100 Guards' tanks and about 2,500 15th Scottish infantry. And, as we have seen, on the right were two complete brigade groups of 43rd Wessex Division. Just west of Cleve were four more battalions of 15th Scottish and most of the artillery of two divisions. The Cleve area was, after all, where XXX Corps' main thrust was to be made.

Allied Intelligence had accurately assessed the available German reserves and the time it would take to bring them into action; the floods were still rising and the road to Calcar runs along only slightly raised ground: time was the most important factor, for every hour the advance east was delayed gave the Germans time to establish a replacement defence line.

During the night the Seaforth's patrols reported that the Germans were withdrawing from Hasselt and the next day the battalion went back but without their tanks. Patrols got through the rapidly rising floods and discovered that the Germans had blocked the way by occupying a wood through which the road ran some 1,200 yards ahead. The next objective was Moyland, two miles from Hasselt and three from Calcar, and a full brigade attack with three battalions of infantry and a battalion of tanks was planned for its capture the following day, 14th February.

The floods now reached their highest levels and the main axis, the Nijmegen-Cleve road was closed to all traffic. Miracles of improvisation on the part of the supply services kept the machine going – '15th Divisional "Q" organised a DUKW service while Corps took over responsibility for the supply of ammunition and petrol. Miraculously, no unit was to go short through all the fighting ahead,' says the official historian of the 15th Scottish. 'A DUKW point for the Brigade was established at the railway station in Nijmegen and each battalion was allowed to make two trips daily. This taxi service worked perfectly and the battalions never once went short of petrol, food or ammunition,' is the tribute paid by the historian of the 6th Guards Tank Brigade.

Nevertheless the floods, both man-made and those caused by the exceptionally heavy rainfall, were Germany's most powerful weapon in slowing down the Allies' great blow through the Reichswald and the hours thus gained gave them time to recover from the chaos created by the tremendous weight of the attack and to bring in forces to create a new defence line.

The going so far had been sticky for the Allies; it was going to become even stickier.

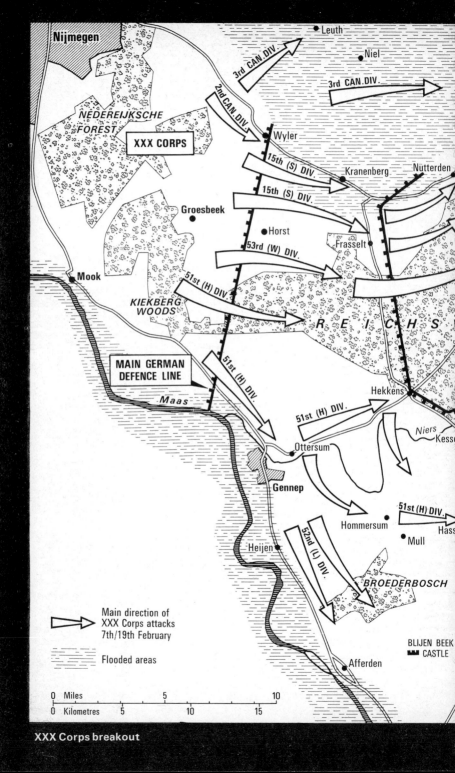

XXX Corps breakout

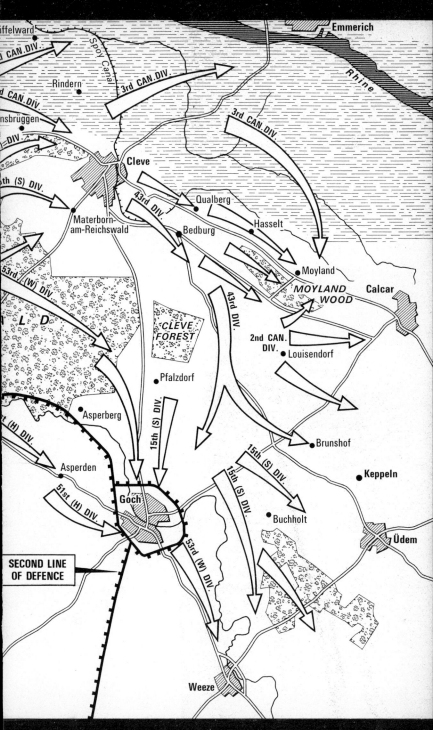

Emmerich

Rhine

iffelward

Spoy Canal

1 CAN. DIV.

3rd CAN. DIV.

3rd CAN. DIV.

Rindern

d CAN. DIV.

nsbrüggen

DIV.

Cleve

5th (S) DIV.

43rd DIV.

Qualberg

Hasselt

Materborn-am-Reichswald

Bedburg

Moyland

53rd (W) DIV.

43rd DIV.

MOYLAND WOOD

Calcar

L D

CLEVE FOREST

2nd CAN. DIV.

Louisendorf

Pfalzdorf

Asperberg

15th (S) DIV.

Brunshof

Keppeln

(H) DIV.

Asperden

15th (S) DIV.

15th (S) DIV.

Goch

Buchholt

Üdem

51st (H) DIV.

53rd (W) DIV.

SECOND LINE OF DEFENCE

Weeze

Defence 'at all costs'

The man entrusted by Field-Marshal von Rundstedt with the task of stopping the Allies' attack through the Reichswald was *General der Panzertruppen* Heinrich Freiherr von Lüttwitz, one of the most experienced mechanized warfare commanders in the German Army, who had a well-deserved reputation for drive and audacity. His XLVII Panzer Corps, the Wehrmacht's 'No. 1 Reserve', had fought all over north-west Europe since the invasion and was respected by all five Allied armies it had encountered.

By February 1945 XLVII Panzer Corps was far from the shatteringly powerful mixed force which in December had crashed through the First US Army's front in the Battle of the Bulge but it consisted of two of the best armoured divisions in the Wehrmacht, the 116th Panzer and the 15th Panzer Grenadier, and its headquarters were immensely experienced. Although Lüttwitz had only fifty tanks against the 5–600 theoretically available to the three British divisions he was about to encounter there were other factors that went a long way to redress the apparent overwhelming Allied superiority.

As we have seen the mud and flood very seriously curtailed the movement of tanks through and around the Reichswald – the Shermans in particular, with their narrower tracks, found the thick mud impassable. Also Lüttwitz's armour was able to operate from the protection of the Siegfried Line defences sited to face open ground offering no cover for tanks. Finally there was the undeniable and, to the Allied tank crews, bitter fact that in the sixth year of the war German tanks were still greatly superior to American or British. A single, well-placed Tiger or Panther with its high-velocity gun, could and often did, hold up many Shermans whose short-barreled 75s had half the range and penetration

Mortar crew

power. The self-propelled 88mm anti-tank gun, adapted from an anti-aircraft gun, could knock out a Sherman from nearly two miles and was absolutely deadly – even against the frontal armour – to any Allied tank at a mile, from where it was still beyond the tank's range.

The XLVII Panzer Corps were equipped with Mk IVs, Mk Vs, a few Mk VIs and self-propelled guns as well as mobile anti-aircraft guns, towed 88s, multi-barreled mortars and automatic weapons. Mk IVs were in the majority, for this well-tried mainstay of German armour was still being produced in large numbers. It was equipped with a long-barreled 75mm gun, at least the equal of the Allies' best tank gun, and was fast, manoeuvrable and rugged. The Mk V 'Panther' was the best German tank with its high-velocity 75mm gun, its thick armour, sloping front plate, twelve-cylinder, 700 horsepower engine and reliable seven-speed gearbox. The Mk VI 'Tiger', built to carry the magnificent 88mm – the outstanding gun of the Second World War – was twenty-five per cent heavier than the Panther but its engine was slightly smaller so that it was slower and much more unwieldy. German tank men did not like it and referred to it as a 'furniture wagon'.

But undoubtedly the most dangerous threat to the British tanks that 15th Panzer Grenadiers possessed was the *Jagd-panther*. This was an 88mm high-velocity anti-tank gun carried in a turretless Panther. It was a late development – only 382 were ever manufactured – but had proved itself to be the Wehrmacht's best anti-tank weapon.

Lüttwitz thought that the Allied offensive between the Waal and the Maas, aimed at crossing the Rhine, showed many resemblances to the German December offensive in the Ardennes, aimed at crossing the Meuse. Like the Battle of the Bulge, Veritable had hurled a mixed armoured and infantry force against a narrow, weakly-held front with the obvious intention of a quick tactical breakthrough followed by deep strategic penetration. Like the German offensive the British one had been unable to break clear in the critical first three days and the defenders had been granted time to bring in their reserve.

But Lüttwitz, whose panzer corps had progressed further than any other in the Battle of the Ardennes, considered that the Americans in the northern half of the Bulge, under Montgomery, had erred in concentrating on creating a defence line and should have used their great armoured strength in a counter-attack as soon as it was available. He was determined not to repeat that mistake.

His first plan was to attack through the shattered German 84th Infantry Division and recapture Cleve and the high ground to the west of it, but at Üdem he learned that the British had already reached Hau (43rd Wessex) and were at the eastern edge of the Reichswald about to cut the Cleve-Goch road (53rd Welsh). German Intelligence also reported the large numbers of British tanks, some with the new high velocity, 17-pounder guns. Lüttwitz decided therefore to send both his divisions westward into the Reichswald, where the Allied superiority in armour and artillery would be less effective. First steps were for existing forces to block the way to Calcar while 116th Panzer Division drove west through Bedburg and 15th Panzer Grenadiers cleared the area from Cleve Forest down to the West Wall defences in the south-eastern quarter of the Reichswald.

It was here, it will be remembered, that the 53rd Welsh Division planned to push forward their two leading brigades on 12th February to the eastern edge of the forest. German counter-attacks had been beaten off during the night of 11th/12th, and early in the morning, on 158th Brigade's front (on the division's centre and right), the 1/5 Welch Regiment, which had been stopped about a quarter of a mile short of the Cleve-Asperden road the night before, renewed its advance against stubborn resistance in which the supporting tanks incurred heavy casualties. The road was gained by midday but by then only four of the sixteen Shermans of 9th RTR were still in action.

On 158th Brigade's left the leading battalions of 160th Brigade also continued their advance. At dawn on 12th February the 2nd Monmouthshire Regiment passed through the overnight positions of the 4th Welch and cleared the north-east corner of the Reichswald; on their right the 6th Royal Welch Fusiliers advanced to the Cleve-Asperden road. But when the 4th Welch were ordered to continue the advance by leap-frogging the RWF they met the first of a series of violent counter-attacks. When the commander of the leading company was killed the regiment's colonel took over personally and, using two companies, restored the situation. Forty Germans were captured and 4th Welch pushed on, digging in east of the important Cleve-Goch road.

Although they did not immediately realise it the advance units of the 53rd had run head on into two battle groups of 15th Panzer Grenadier Division. Early in the afternoon of 12th February elements from 115th Panzer Grenadier and 104th Panzer Grenadier Regiments with artillery, mortar and self-propelled guns in support launched a fierce attack at the seam between the 158th and 160th Brigade Groups.

The men of the 6th Royal Welch Fusiliers and of the 1/5th Welch Regiment, warned by the preliminary shelling and mortar fire, were ready for the attack when it came in. They held their fire until the panzer grenadiers were less than 300 yards away and when the order was at last given the resulting hail of bullets caused heavy casualties and the attack broke up in confusion. Farther south the

East Lancs beat off one attack and, when a second seemed about to come in, called for an artillery 'stonk'. Most of the division's guns responded and the assault force scattered.

By nightfall of the 12th February the 53rd Welsh Division had two brigades along a line running from the Cleve-Goch road (at the point where the extreme north-east corner of the Reichswald is cut by the road) south-west to the Cleve-Asperden road just north of a crossroads 1,000 yards from the Asperberg bridge. On 53rd's left, contact had been made with 43rd Wessex Division in the Hau and Bedburg area and on the right 51st Highland Division's 7th Argylls were positioned in the Reichswald north-east of Kessel. This still left the south-east corner of the Reichswald, in which there was a north-south line of anti-tank ditch and concrete emplacements, to clear before the advance on Goch could take place.

All of 53rd Division's infantry battalions had taken casualties during the five days' almost continual action and the supporting armour of 34th Armoured Brigade had been very roughly handled: the 9th Royal Tank Regiment, which had lost thirty-eight out of fifty-two tanks, had to be withdrawn for refitting and re-organising and the 141st RAC were reduced to about half strength. Anti-tank guns were brought up to compensate for the loss of armour.

But with the German strength visibly increasing from hour to hour it was imperative, if the initiative were not to be lost, that the momentum of the advance be maintained and it was decided that 53rd Welsh would have to continue their attacks the next day and clear the Reichswald despite the cost. The plan was to bring up the reserve brigade – the 71st, who had been mopping up behind – reinforced by 1/5th Welch from 158th Brigade and what was left of 141st RAC, and clear the forest in the centre as far as the Cleve-Asperden road. On the right the rest of 158th Brigade were to swing right, clear the south-eastern strip of forest down to the river Niers and, if possible, capture the Asperberg bridge intact. On division left the 160th Brigade would hold ground won and mop up.

The 158th Brigade attack went in first. Shortly after daybreak of 13th February a reconnaissance squadron led the 7th Royal Welch Fusiliers east through the quarter-mile wide strip of forest to within a few hundred yards of the bridge where they came under heavy fire from a strong German position dug in on high ground. The 7th RWF attacked vigorously but despite committing all its battalions in a fight that went on all day and cost them a further seventy casualties were unable to crack the German position. A loud explosion told them that their hopes of capturing the bridge intact were gone and this was confirmed by aerial reconnaissance the next day. The position was stalemate and it was decided to mount a heavy attack on the bridge site three days later when the 51st Highland Division would attack Asperden south of the river.

The attack of 71st Brigade in the centre went much better mainly because a heavy artillery barrage took some of the starch out of the Germans and because the 1st Highland Light Infantry and the 4th Royal Welch Fusiliers were comparatively fresh and the prospect of at last getting clear of the forest was an added spur. By noon all objectives had been reached at a cost of only thirty casualties.

The 53rd Division's initial role had ended. They had fought in appalling conditions for six days and five nights and had broken through two lines of West Wall defences, and at the end of an exhausting advance, had met the full fury of two battle groups of a fresh German armoured division and pushed them back, knocking out eight 88mm guns, large numbers of mortars and machine guns, several Mk IV tanks and four of the *Jagd panthers*.

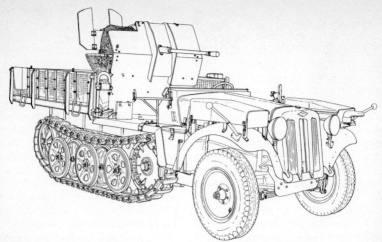

One of the great problems with light anti-aircraft guns was their lack of mobility, especially as this hampered the Germans in their efforts to shoot down appreciable numbers of the Allied fighter bombers and light bombers roaming the skies of Germany at low level towards the end of the war. The obvious answer, and the easiest one, was to mount these light pieces on half tracks, which could move the weapons about quickly, but which would not require much time to get back into action. Illustrated here is a Model 38 20mm cannon mounted on an Sdkfz 10 1 ton half track, one of the many conversions undertaken by the Germans late in the war

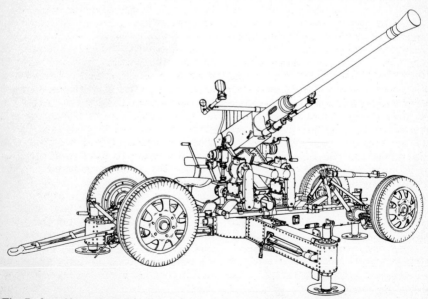

The Bofors 40mm Anti-Aircraft Gun was one of the war's most widely used weapons. Designed before the war in Sweden, it was built in great quantities in Great Britain, and was continuously updated. In action it weighed 2.4 tons, needed a crew of about six, and could fire a 2-pound shell at the rate of 120 rounds per minute to an effective altitude of 12,000 feet

The one bright spot on XXX Corps' hard-fighting front had been on 14th February when the sun shone from a brilliantly clear sky. 'Visibility unlimited' was the met. report and the Allied air forces responded magnificently. Within twenty-four hours over 9,000 sorties were flown along the battle front, immediately behind it or deep into Germany. Above the fighting troops 'cab ranks' of rocket-firing Typhoons or eight-machine-gun Spitfires were 'on call' and some thirty-two attacks were made just ahead of the infantry. It was all immensely heartening to the troops who had been slogging through mud and rain for a week but the next day the weather closed in again enabling the Germans to move their armour.

The 15th Panzer Grenadiers, as well as trying to stop the advance through the Reichswald, had despatched a third battle group from Üdem northwest to occupy the high ground between the southern edge of Moyland Wood (116th Panzer Division's left) and the north-east corner of Cleve Forest. This move was completed by the night of 12th February so that 15th Panzer Grenadier tanks, self-propelled guns, mortar batteries and machine-gun positions lay right across 43rd Wessex Division's projected line of advance.

On 13th February 43rd's 129th Brigade launched their attack to seize the ridge south-east of Bedburg needed as a start line for the advance south. The assault was made by the 5th Wiltshire Regiment who, almost immediately, came under heavy shell fire but despite grievous casualties kept moving forward and gained the ridge.

In the afternoon the divisional artillery turned every available gun on the country ahead and 4th Wiltshire, supported by 8th Armoured Brigade, advanced from the ridge. One by one the tanks bogged down in the deep mud. The infantry went on without them and despite mortar shelling and machine-gun fire fought

their way into the objective, the small village of Trippenberg, by nightfall. Here, without armour or anti-tank guns, they awaited the inevitable counter-attack.

It came at dawn on 14th February with a combined panzer and panzer grenadier assault on the village supported by 88mm air bursts. One company of 4th Wiltshire was overrun but the rest hung on and stopped the German attack. At 11.0am 5th Wiltshire, who had remained on the ridge 1,000 yards behind during the night, tried to resume the advance but came under heavy fire from machine-guns, mortars and 88s. The centre and left hand companies were pinned down but the one on the right kept going only to run into an equal number of panzer grenadiers. Stiff hand-to-hand fighting broke out, the shelling and mortaring seemed to increase and soon every senior 4th Wiltshire officer except one was a casualty. The wounded commanding officer ordered the battalion to 'dig in and hold' and not until a new commanding officer got up to the battalion about 3.0pm did he allow himself to be evacuated.

As darkness fell the survivors of the 5th Wiltshire were on the point of exhaustion but the new commanding officer decided that the attack must be continued through the night in order to secure a start line for the division's reserve brigade, the 130th, who had passed through 53rd Welsh Division ready to take over the lead from the badly-battered 129th Brigade.

Fighting their way through the dark and without artillery support 5th Wiltshire pushed the Germans back from their forward positions and wrested from them the key crossroads a quarter of a mile from the north-east corner of Cleve Forest, despite concentrated machine-gun fire. Dawn of 15th February found them firm upon their objective but they had lost 200 men. The 4th Wiltshire's losses had been almost as heavy. Nevertheless 43rd Wessex re-

The formidable Jagdpanther

solved to continue the advance towards the high ground overlooking Goch without a break and the reserve brigade were ordered to attack the next day, 15th February.

The 130th Infantry Brigade consisted of the 7th Royal Hampshire, the 4th and the 5th Dorset Regiments. Early on the 15th the 4th Dorset Regiment moved through the positions recently won by the 5th Wiltshire and advanced in the face of shell, mortar and Spandau fire. In five hours they had pushed forward to yet another ridge – sometimes after three attempts to clear a particularly well-held position. Immediately the 7th Royal Hampshires were passed through and continued the attack. Heavy machine-gun fire poured into their flank from Cleve Forest but the fighting went on all through the night and the advance continued with the 5th Dorsets taking over the lead about midnight.

At 9.30am on 16th February a fresh attack carried 130th Brigade on to a ridge between Louisendorf and Cleve Forest. The 214th Brigade Group, who had been halted since their fierce fight for Hau on 12th February, were now hurrying south from the Bedburg area to take over the lead and try to smash through to a line running east from Pfalzdorf, three miles north of Goch, to Schroershof, five miles north-east of Goch on the road to Calcar. From this line the next and final move would be to the escarpment immediately north of Goch.

While this heavy fighting had been going on in the centre of the battlefield the divisions on the flanks had had their share of trouble, particularly the 15th Scottish in the north attempting to capture Calcar.

The all-out assault against the German blocking position some three quarters of a mile east of Hasselt was to be made on 14th February with all three of 46th Highland Brigade's battalions: the 7th Seaforths from Hasselt, the 9th Cameronians on their

stream tanks advanced through the centre of Moyland Wood and through the village of Rosendahl without much difficulty but at a cluster of houses called Tillesmanskath, 1,000 yards farther on, bitter opposition was encountered which included shelling, mortar fire, self-propelled guns and spandau. The leading company took very heavy casualties and were reduced to forty men by the time they tried to take their objective, a knoll astride a sunken lane south of the houses. The Germans' parachute infantry counter-attacked and the Glasgow Highlanders were driven back and the survivors had to be withdrawn under cover of smoke. The other two companies pulled back into the deep wooded gullies and the tanks, which were of little use in such close country, were withdrawn.

On 46th Brigade's left the Seaforths and their supporting Coldstream tanks set out, two companies up, along the flood-covered road at 9.30am on 14th February. The Churchills which could not, of course, leave the road, were soon stopped by mines and when the infantry tried to advance without armoured protection they suffered severe casualties. The leading company's commander was killed by machine-gun fire.

The Seaforth's pioneers, working under continuous shell-fire, slowly and efficiently lifted the mines and cleared a path for the tanks who moved up and used their big guns against the houses manned by the Germans. The artillery added their fire power and the Seaforths rushed the Germans. They captured twenty-three machine guns and consolidated north-east of Rosendahl for the night. Patrols discovered the Germans strongly entrenched west of Moyland and it was plain that 15th Scottish would be faced with very heavy fighting on the morrow.

At the other end of the front the 51st Highland Division had driven the Germans off the high ground south of Gennep from which heavy and

left and the 2nd Glasgow Highlanders on their right but when reconnaissance from these last two battalions tried to move up to the Seaforths at first light they found that the flood had now risen to the tops of the hedges and the Seaforths were marooned on the 'island' of Hasselt. The Cameronians and the Glasgow Highlanders were therefore diverted south to Bedburg behind the 43rd Wessex and launched south-eastward 'to find the enemy and destroy him.'

About 1.30pm the Cameronians and No. 1 Squadron of the Coldstream Guards, the right hand formation, advanced against little opposition along the axis of the road which runs south of Moyland Wood. By 4.30pm they had made over a mile and a half and taken thirty prisoners. As they were some 600 yards ahead of any other 46th Brigade troops they were ordered to halt and consolidate for the night.

The centre and left formations had not had things quite so easy. The Glasgow Highlanders with more Cold-

The PzKw VI Tiger II was undoubtedly the best tank produced by the Germans in the Second World War, especially in its turret design, gun-power and armour. There were two turret designs, one by Henschel and one by Porsche, and both had thick and excellently sloped armour. Production was greatly hampered by the continued Allied air and land offensives into Germany, but the few hundred that were produced amply proved their value. In action, the Tiger II was let down by the fact that it was unreliable, not very manoeuvrable and underpowered, but these were partially counterbalanced by the fact that the tank was intended for the defensive role, in which it did not have to move far. *Weight:* 68½ tons. *Crew:* 5 *Armament:* one 88mm KwK 43/L 71 gun with 78 rounds and two 7.92mm machine guns with 5,850 rounds. *Speed:* 26mph (road) and 13mph (cross country) *Range:* up to 106 miles. *Armour:* lower front and turret front 100mm, upper front 150mm, sides 80mm and top 40mm

The Jagdpanther was produced in 1943 (first going into action in 1944) in an
effort to produce a viable tank destroyer. The new vehicle resulted from the
marriage of the 88-mm PAK 43 anti-aircraft and anti-tank gun and the chassis of the
Pzkw V Panther tank. The chassis remained basically unaltered, the front and side
plates being extended upwards to form the strong and well sloped hull which
carried the gun. *Crew:* 5. *Weight:* 46 tons *Speed:* 28.5mph (road), 15mph (cross
country). *Length overall:* 33 feet 3 inches *Width:* 10 feet 10 inches. *Height:* 8 feet
11 inches. *Armament:* one 88mm gun with 60 rounds and one 7.92mm machine gun.
Armour: 60mm (lower nose), 80mm (front plate), 50mm (sides), 40mm (rear, hull
and superstructure) and 120mm (mantlet)

accurate fire had been directed against their Niers crossings but the loss of Gennep had been seen to be a tactical disaster by General Straube, whose LXXXVI Corps was now responsible for the defence of Goch, for once the Allies had secured a firm base south of the Niers they would be able to mount an attack towards Goch from the south-west coinciding with ones that were obviously coming in from the west and the north. Straube ordered two companies of infantry and a battery of self-propelled 88s to move from the Siegfried Line defences and recapture Gennep.

On 13th February after the 88s had heavily shelled the Gordons' forward positions the German infantry attacked with great determination.

A knocked out Tiger

Only rapid and accurate 3-inch mortar fire stopped them overrunning the Gordon's line. The German commander reported that Gennep was strongly held by a mixed force of armour, self-propelled guns and 'Grade One' infantry and was allowed to withdraw to the Broederbosch, a wood some two miles south.

Also on 13th February 51st Highland were reinforced by the infantry complement of the Guards Armoured Division, the 32nd Guards Brigade, it being apparent that conditions made the use of the Guards' tanks impossible for the time being. The 32nd Guards Brigade consisted of a battalion each of the Coldstream, the Irish, and the Welsh Guards and for its role in Veritable the brigade was reinforced with a second battalion of Welsh Guards, the West Somerset Yeomanry and a battery of the 21st Anti-tank Regiment.

Their objective was the village of Hommersum about three miles southeast of Gennep. This entailed clearing a small wood south-east of Gennep first and at 3.30pm on 14th February the 5th Battalion Coldstream Guards and the 1st Battalion Welsh Guards carried out this task capturing a few dozen German paratroopers and losing two or three of their own men to mines. The 3rd Battalion Irish Guards then passed through and seized Hommersum with little difficulty. Seventy-eight prisoners were taken and the Guards Armoured Division were informed that their troops were 'in Germany'.

Although the Germans had given up the idea of recapturing Gennep they were determined that the Allies were not to be allowed to expand their offensive south-east along the east bank of the Maas. A new defensive line was formed by LXXXVI Corps running east from the Maas along a *beek*, which had been enlarged into an anti-tank ditch and flooded, to Blijen Beek Castle, surrounded by a moat. This line lay just south of the Broederbosch woods and included the small village of Afferden on the banks of the Maas.

Exploitation in this direction was now the responsibility of a new infantry division committed from the reserve, the 52nd Lowland who were put in on the right of the British line on February 14th with orders to crack the western hinge of the German defence line.

Meanwhile 51st Highland Division

were free to devote all their attention to the attack on Goch and for this it was necessary to bring 154th Brigade, in the Hekkens area, across the Niers to capture Kessel so the advance could continue on a two brigade front.

The Niers bridge south of Hekkens was found, not unexpectedly, to have been blown and once more 79th Division's Buffaloes were called upon to ferry the infantry across. The place chosen was a bend in the river where it came right up to the Gennep-Hekkens road and here during the night of 13/14th February two assault companies of the Black Watch were carried over and a second battalion plus stores etc. on the next day. On the same day, 14th February, the 7th Argyll and Sutherland Highlanders were ferried across and, moving through the Black Watch bridgehead, assaulted Kessel which they took with seventy prisoners.

Now with the Niers behind them and their right flank protected 51st Highland Division were ready for the last phase of their operation, the advance to their final objective, Goch.

On the night of the 16th/17th February the 53rd Welsh Division started their final attack in the Battle of the Reichswald. Moving out of the southeast corner of the forest the 71st Infantry Brigade's 1st Oxfordshire and Buckinghamshire Light Infantry and the 7th Royal Welch Fusiliers attacked at night behind a very heavy rolling barrage to clear the bridge site area near Asperberg and the roads running east and north-east from it. Because of the strength of the resistance earlier encountered around the blown bridge five Medium Regiments of Artillery fired a half hour preliminary bombardment on the whole area. This was followed by a barrage fired by four Field and three Medium Regiments. Not for the first time some of these shells fell short causing casualties to the RWF but the effect of the rolling barrage was to keep the Germans in their trenches and cellars and both battalions were

on their objectives within two hours.

Then, however, parties of Germans who had been by-passed in the dark came out and fired on support troops moving up. One party of anti-tank guns, signallers, stretcher bearers and ammunition carriers were practically wiped out by heavy fire from dug-in Germans. Heavy fighting then broke out in Asperberg and once again the Germans were able to inflict damage quite out of proportion to their numbers. Eight young paratroopers armed with Spandaus charged forward firing from the hip in the best film tradition and although they were all killed their example made it necessary to clear the rest out house by house and it was not until 7.0am on 17th February that the brigade was firmly established. The advance had cost them seventy-three casualties.

On the 17th February the 160th Brigade cleared the whole area between the Reichswald and Cleve Forests against no opposition; on the 18th the 71st Brigade closed up between the 43rd and 51st Divisions attacking Goch. 53rd Welsh Division's role in the Battle of the Reichswald was over. It had been their hardest battle of the Second World War. In it they lost nearly a third of the 10,000 casualties they suffered in the war. But their successful attacking advance through the Reichswald Forest in the conditions of the time was an outstanding feat of arms which contributed greatly to the eventual breaking of the very strong German defence lines.

The week's hard, disappointing fighting had been exhausting and costly for XXX Corps. It had also, human beings being what they are, brought about recriminations and accusations between units at all levels up to divisions. Some felt they had been let down, had had to do more than their share or were being asked to take on unreasonably large tasks Among the difficulties of the great set-piece attack, which was the mark of Montgomery, is that if its promise of an almost mechanical advance is not fulfilled the resulting disappointment in command at the top is bad for morale. If there is a major upset in the timing for achieving objectives, thus making the original schedule impossible, the rigidity imposed by the tight interlocking of forces restrains flexibility and it becomes difficult to put a new plan quickly into operation.

As soon as Horrocks had recovered from his attack of fever he made it a daily practice to visit key divisional and brigade headquarters, not, he says, to urge them on or to attempt to interfere with local command, but by giving them an opportunity to let off steam by getting complaints off their chests, and by giving them what encouraging news he could of successes on other parts of the front, to lift morale.

On his part General Crerar made constant flights over the battlefield in a small observation aircraft and visited Horrocks' headquarters daily with a very clear picture of how the battle was progressing. Crerar and Horrocks have stressed that the Battle of the Reichswald was fought by the regimental commanders because the state of communications made close control at any higher level virtually impossible.

Both Crerar and Horrocks were well aware that the floods, the collapse of communications, the virtual grounding of the air force and, above all, the cancellation of Grenade had profoundly changed the scope of Veritable which would have to be a slog against increasing resistance instead of a quick break-through to the Rhine. So far the Canadian involvement had been largely defensive and the reserve armour, both British and Canadian, had been stymied by mud and flood. It was a time for new command decisions.

Simonds, Canadian II Corps' commander, proposed employing his infantry divisions and their supporting armour and artillery in an attack north from the Nijmegen area to cross the Lower Rhine west of Arnhem, wheel right and drive up the Rhine along its right bank. This bold suggestion was turned down by Crerar who, while admitting its attractions, refused to be diverted from 'completing what we have set out to do in Veritable.'

Although Goch had not fallen, Cleve had, and XXX Corps' four divisions were through the Reichswald Forest and had broadened their assault front from the original cramped six miles to fourteen. Both defensive flanks were protected by two more divisions, the 3rd Canadian on the left and the 52nd Lowland on the right. Water and mud still severely limited deployment but Crerar decided that the time had come to bring a second corps into the battle and on 14th February he told Horrocks and Simonds that he was dividing the front into two with XXX Corps on the right and II Canadian Corps on the left.

Horrocks' immediate objective was Goch, the German anchor position, and after that had been broken XXX Corps would thrust south-west on two axes: on the right down the east bank of the Maas from Gennep to Venlo; on the left from Goch through Weeze and Kevelaer to Geldern. The II Canadian Corps' immediate objective was to seize Calcar and then drive south-west along two more axes: Marienbaum-Xanten and through Üdem towards the Xanten-Geldern road. But on 14th February detailed planning went no further than the capture of Goch and Calcar.

On their part the Germans were well aware of the importance of Goch in the defence of the Rhineland and designated it, like Calcar, an 'at all costs' defensive position. More reinforcements, artillery and self-propelled guns were found and the crippled Luftwaffe were ordered in to the attack.

For the Allied troops between the floods of the Rhine and the Maas the hardest fighting still lay ahead.

The defence is cracked at last

When the command changes became effective on 15th February 3rd Canadian Division reverted to Simonds' corps (2nd Canadian had already done so) and the 46th Highland Brigade was also placed temporarily under Canadian command. The rest of the 15th Scottish Division were withdrawn into XXX Corps reserve to rest and refit in preparation for their part in the capture of Goch.

The corps boundary was the Bedburg-Üdem road and because of the extensive flooding on the left this meant that II Canadian Corps had a very narrow front. Simonds could only bring one brigade at a time into battle and he started with 3rd Division's 7th Infantry who, with the tanks of the Scots Guards, were to pass through 46th Highland Brigade's positions in Moyland Woods and open the way to Calcar.

Simonds' other division, 2nd Canadian, who, it will be remembered, had been squeezed out of the battle at the end of the first day's fighting, were moved up to the Cleve area to be ready to take over the advance from 3rd Division at the right moment. For the time being the Canadian armour, the Fort Garry Horse, were held in reserve.

On the right hand half of the front Horrocks regrouped for the attack on Goch. Right flank protection was entrusted to the 52nd Lowland Division and the infantry of the Guards Armoured Division, the 32nd Guards Brigade. The 51st Highland Division were to advance south of the Niers River and attack the southern half of Goch; 43rd Wessex in the north were to drive south-south-east to cut the important Goch-Calcar road and then south to the escarpment overlooking Goch. Finally 15th Scottish and their supporting 6th Guards Tank Brigade would move through 43rd Wessex to seize the northern half of Goch.

Because of the importance of Calcar

United States gun emplacements begin to fire across the Roer

on the approach to the Rhine the Germans had fiercely resisted every attempt by 15th Scottish to move eastwards from Hasselt or from Bedburg. On 46th Highland Brigade's left the Seaforth Highlanders had been stopped by German infantry, mortar, machine-gun and self-propelled guns ensconced in a small wood just east of Hasselt straddling the road to Moyland. On the brigade centre the Glasgow Highlanders had been pinned down by heavy fire in Moyland Woods just south of the village of Tillemanskath. On the right the Cameronians had met little opposition but had been halted by the brigade commander when they had advanced about a mile and a half east of Bedburg during the night of 14th/15th February.

Because they were comparatively fresh they were ordered to wheel left the next day and 'eliminate opposition on Glasgow Highlanders' front'. This would entail driving the Germans off two knolls in Moyland Woods.

When they attacked on 15th February the Cameronians ran into very heavy rifle and machine-gun fire and found, not surprisingly, that German mortars were zeroed on every track that approached their position. Persevering against mounting losses they managed to capture twenty-five prisoners, dig in on the westernmost knoll by 5.0pm and beat off a determined German counter-attack shortly afterwards.

On the same day the Seaforth Highlanders on the left worked their way forward, swung right and by nightfall were in Tillemanskath. These two successes enabled the hard-pressed Glasgow Highlanders in the centre to straighten out their line. Because the German resistance was so tough the Highland Light Infantry from 227th Brigade, who were supposed to be resting for the attack on Goch, were moved up in Kangaroos to secure the right flank of 46th Highland Brigade left open by the commitment of the Cameronians.

The HLI advanced eastwards in the dark and swirling mist which cut visibility so badly that the tanks had to be sent back. A little later all the accompanying guns bogged down. Pushing on alone for about a mile the leading two companies gathered up eighty prisoners and reached their objectives, two clusters of houses a half mile apart. Here they were almost immediately strongly counter-attacked and the right-hand company, caught silhouetted against the flames of burning houses, were cut down and thrown back with heavy casualties.

On the following day, 16th February, the HLI's reserve tried to clear the eastern extension of Moyland Woods but the German machine-gun fire was so intense that their assault was stopped almost at its start line. On their left the Cameronians flung themselves against the easternmost knoll and after a fierce fight among the trees about half the company gained the heights and dug in in time to resist repeated German counter-attacks preceded by exceptionally heavy mortaring. With the help of Wasp flame-throwers, another Cameronian company finally fought its way to the south-eastern corner of the main wood. The Germans now fell back across the road running south from Moyland and concentrated in the eastern extension of the woods. From here they were able to put down such heavy fire on the road and on the track running along the southern edge of their wood that 46th Highland Brigade's troops could advance no further.

On 16th February the Canadian 7th Infantry Brigade Group added their weight to the attacks eastward from the Bedburg area. On the left the Regina Rifle Regiment, supported by a squadron of Scots Guards' tanks tried to clear the troublesome eastern extension of Moyland Wood; on the right the Royal Winnipeg Rifles and two squadrons of Scots Guards' Churchills were sent to clear high ground in the Louisendorf area.

Although the north-east corner of Moyland Wood had been reported clear by 46th Highland Brigade the Regina Rifles came under heavy flanking fire from it when they tried to advance north and had to spend most of the 16th in clearing it. The Germans, some of 346th Fusilier Battalion and the 60th Panzer Grenadier Regiment, fell back into the final defensive position before Calcar, the eastern extension of Moyland Woods, where their machine-guns, added to those already in position, were able to stop the Regina Rifles from crossing the road.

On the Canadian right the Royal Winnipeg Rifles, mounted in Kanga-roos and supported by Scots Guards' tanks, advanced in a hail of shell-fire and multiple rockets from newly-arrived German reinforcements. The Kangaroos slowed down but the tanks pushed on and reached Louisendorf alone. The village was then subjected to almost continuous shelling and the Canadian infantry were understand-ably reluctant to dismount from the protection of the Kangaroos until a captain of the Scots Guards left his tank and walked from one carrier to another at the height of the shelling, getting many of the infantry out and guiding them to their positions before he was killed.

An hour and a half after the tanks had entered Louisendorf the RWR came in and by dark were firmly established both in the village and on the high ground to the north which the second tank squadron had been hol-ding alone for two hours.

Slit trenches were dug and the tanks placed over them. Under this protec-tion the infantry slept, after sending back some 240 prisoners, and despite the shelling which went on all night not one soldier was hit.

The next morning, 17th February, the Regina Rifles and Scots Guards' tanks renewed their efforts to clear the last bit of Moyland Wood but heavy artillery and mortar fire proved too much for them. The 88mm high-explosive shells were detonated by the tops of the trees, raining white-hot pieces of metal on the troops below. The attack could make no headway and at 4.0pm, under cover of smoke, the infantry and tanks withdrew.

The right hand attack by the Canadian's reserve, the 1st Canadian Scottish, and a squadron of Scots Guards' tanks advanced through heavy machine-gun and shell fire eastwards to seize important high ground half a mile south of the eastern end of the grimly-defended Moyland Woods. 150 paratroopers were captured but the Canadians suffered many casualties. One Scots Guards' tank broke down and had to be towed back but the suspicion that the driver had not been doing his maintenance was forgotten when an armour piercing 88mm shell was found nestling in the transmission.

The going on the north flank was proving to be extraordinarily difficult as the Germans fought back fiercely, skilfully and with conspicuous courage. Almost the only weapon which ever caused them to break in panic were the flame-throwers. More troops kept coming in to hold the line in front of Calcar and heavy field guns were moved up north of the Rhine and added their shells to the continual bombardment of the Allied attackers.

The failure to clear Moyland Woods had seriously upset 2nd Canadian Corps' plans and on the 18th one more attempt was made by the Regina Rifle Regiment with flame-throwers to clear the last area, the eastern extension. The Germans were slowly pushed northwards but only from the western half of the wood. In the other half, an area only a 1,000 yards long and 500 wide, the Germans threw back every attempt. At the end of the day the Regina Rifles casualties had risen to a hundred and the way to Calcar was still blocked.

All this time the 2nd Canadian Division had been waiting in the Cleve area to exploit 3rd Divisions'

breakthrough and now it was decided to hold the line on the left and commit 2nd Division's 4th Infantry Brigade, supported by the tanks of the Fort Garry Horse, on the right.

While the Canadians had been grimly fighting for every yard of ground in the north, XXX Corps troops had been meeting equally fanatical resistance on their front. The fresh 52nd Lowland Division on the extreme right attacked with confidence on 16th February from south of Gennep along the east bank of the Maas to capture Afferden and cross an anti-tank ditch which ran east from the river and included a moated, mediaeval castle.

The main German defensive position before the anti-tank ditch was the Broederbosch, some four square miles of woods. This was attacked by the 5th Highland Light Infantry and the 5th King's Own Scottish Borderers but the Germans met them with heavy mortar and machine-gun fire supported by extremely accurate snipers. The reserve battalion, the 7/9th Royal Scots had to be committed before the woods were cleared.

But when, the next day, two battalions of Highland Light Infantry attempted to knock out Blijenbeek Castle with a direct assault they ran into intense fire from well-sited machine-guns and were knocked back with heavy casualties. On the 18th the 4th King's Own Scottish Borderers and Churchill tanks of 34th Armoured Brigade attempted to advance across 700 yards of open ground between the woods and the castle. They were met by fire from guns on higher ground behind the keep and lost many tanks. This attack having failed, a single company tried to rush a breach in the walls. They were cut down like wheat.

Not until the weather cleared and the RAF dropped nine 1,000lb bombs on the castle did it fall and then, to the astonishment of all, it was discovered that the defenders had numbered only fifteen desperate paratroopers who had been kept supplied by rafts pushed across during the

The Panther was perhaps Germany's best tank of the war, and was influenced, as far as design went, by the superlative Russian T-34. This is especially true of the low silhouette and the good sloping of the armour. The Panther was pushed into production very quickly, and therefore suffered from a large crop of teething troubles to begin with, but once these had been sorted out, the tank was more than a match for Allied vehicles. *Crew:* 5. *Weight:* 45.5 tons. *Speed:* 28 mph (road) and 15.5 mph (cross country). *Length overall:* 29 feet $0\frac{3}{4}$ inches. *Width:* 10 feet $8\frac{3}{4}$ inches. *Height:* 9 feet 10 inches. *Armament:* one 75-mm gun with 82 rounds and up to three 7.9-2mm machine guns with 4,200 rounds. *Armour:* 80-mm (front), 110-mm (turret front), 40-mm (side), 15-mm (top) and 40-mm (rear)

The Pzkw IV was one of Germany's mainstays in the tank field throughout the war, and was continually updated in order to meet the increasingly stringent operational demands put upon it. Naturally enough, gunpower was a paramount factor, for initially the Pzkw IV was undergunned. The increase of gunpower reached its culmination in the J model, which was fitted with a long barrelled 75-mm gun. But despite the increase in offensive power, the model was still seriously lacking in defensive power, i.e. its armour. *Crew:* 5. *Weight:* 25 tons. *Speed:* 25 mph (road), 15 mph (cross country). *Length overall:* 23 feet $4\frac{1}{2}$ inches. *Width:* 10 feet $9\frac{1}{2}$ inches (with skirts). *Height:* 8 feet 10 inches. *Armament:* one 7.5-mm KwK 40 with 87 rounds and two 7.92-mm machine guns with 3,150 rounds. *Armour:* 80-mm (front), 50-mm (turret front), 30-mm (sides), 20-mm (rear) and 30-mm (turret rear)

night. Among the slogans written on their walls was *Sieger oder Siberien* (Victory or Siberia) and their fanatical resistance gave proof that the Germans were not going to collapse yet – in fact the 52nd Lowland Division would not cross the anti-tank ditch until 1st March.

On their left the infantry of the Guards Armoured Division resumed their attacks on 16th February pushing south-east from Hommersum to capture Mull. The Coldstream started with the support of Welsh Guards' tanks but once again rain and mud defeated the armour and only two out of nineteen were able to stay with the infantry as far as the objective. Early the next day the Welsh Guards advanced to seize the village of Hassum, a mile and a half further east, to link up with 51st Highland Division.

For nearly a week the two forward battalions of 32nd Guards Brigade were shelled constantly in their slit trenches as the incessant rain turned the ground into thick mud reminiscent of the First World War. But, together with the ground held by the 52nd Lowland Division, the right flank of XXX Corps was a hard shoulder which allowed the other divisions to get on with the capture of Goch.

After dark on 16th February, the 51st Highland Division resumed its advance eastwards. On the extreme right flame-throwers helped the Black Watch seize Hassum railway station while on the Highland Division's centre and left the 152nd Brigade's three battalions moved on Grafenthal, Hervost and Asperden. It was necessary for this last place, on the main road half way between Kessel and Goch, to be hit by rocket-firing Typhoons and 'mattressed' before it fell at midnight. (A 'mattress' was 32 rocket launchers joined together and fired simultaneously.)

The 51st were now in possession of a three mile wide assault front running south from the blown Niers bridge near Asperberg through Asperden. The plan called for the 2nd Seaforth Highlanders to make a crossing over the last and deepest anti-tank ditch, for the sappers to get an AVRE bridge in and then for the Black Watch to lead 153 Brigade into the southern part of Goch. At the same time the two-thirds of the town which lies north of the Niers was to be attacked first by the 43rd Wessex and then by the 15th Scottish Division.

It will be remembered that we left 43rd Division's 214 Brigade hurrying south from Bedburg on 16th February to take over the lead from the 130th Brigade who had secured a start line for the final advance to the Goch escarpment in a fighting advance that continued without a break for twenty-four hours. The leading battalions of 214th Brigade were the 1st Worcestershire and the 7th Somerset Light Infantry and they arrived at the scene of battle just as the ground had been seized but before the Germans had completely withdrawn. As they passed through the exhausted troops of 130th Brigade and started to deploy they were fired upon by every available German gun with deadly accuracy. But, almost immediately 43rd's artillery opened up and laid a carpet of shells ahead of their infantry and tanks. The 214 Brigade began their attack just before 4.0pm on 16th February and by nightfall the Somersets, on the right, had advanced nearly 3,000 yards and the Worcesters on the left had reached their objective.

The Germans, resisting furiously, must have thought that they were due for a respite but there was to be no break in the attack against them, for now the reserve battalion, the 5th Duke of Cornwall's Light Infantry, with a squadron of 4th/7th Dragoon Guards' tanks sped south from Bedburg and, reaching the open ground just seized, split into five columns and in the dark and confusion thrust forward for nearly four more miles to cut the vital Goch-Calcar road at Schroershof. Quickly the brigade consolidated along a two-mile front. It was a crippling blow to the defences

German artillery under light camouflage

of both the German 'at all cost' positions, Goch and Calcar.

It was at this moment, when the German defenders of Goch were at last sure that they had the remaining hours of darkness to prepare themselves for the next assault, that 43rd Wessex Division produced the unexpected, daring move which so often tips the scales in battle. The 214th Brigade's right hand battalion, the 7th Somerset Light Infantry, had seized its objective, the eastern outskirts of Pfalzdorf just as the light was fading. It had been intended for the reserve, the 4th Somersets, to continue the advance the next day but instead it was decided to put in a night attack.

At 11.30pm the battalion moved silently off and the Germans were taken completely by surprise. When they recovered and began to hit back with spandau the Somersets called for artillery support. Heavy shelling of the German positions followed quickly and their commander and sixty-eight men surrendered.

By 5.30am on 17th February the Somersets were consolidated on a 1,000 yard front along the escarpment overlooking Goch. A further 180 prisoners were gathered up. Barely six hours later 7th Somerset came forward with tanks of the 4th/7th Dragoon Guards and continued the advance to the south-east part of the escarpment reaching it by 2.30pm.

Also at 11.30 on the morning of the 17th the 1st Worcestershire Regiment who had cut the Goch-Calcar road on the left, resumed their advance encountering some of the heaviest and most accurate shelling of the war. But by 6.0pm they were able to report that

'they were looking down on the chimneys of Goch along a front of 4,000 yards.'

General Horrocks has described 43rd Wessex Division's remarkable 8,000-yard continual advance as the turning point in the Battle of the Reichswald. From the German point of view the cutting of the link between the defenders in Goch and those in the Moyland Wood-Calcar position plus the British seizure of the Goch northern escarpment meant that a withdrawal to the next line of defence before the Rhine was inevitable. Field-Marshal von Rundstedt, Commander-in-Chief West, personally told Hitler that First Canadian Army's attack was only the opening phase of a great Allied offensive and he predicted that it would soon be followed by a major assault by Ninth US Army from the Venlo-Roermond sector which in turn would be followed by

strong thrusts towards the Rhine by First and Third US Armies. In the face of this massive strength, he pointed out that the most important thing was to maintain a cohesive front. Hitler forbade any directives to army, corps, or divisional commanders which would even imply a falling back to the Rhine. No ground was to be yielded; the Allies would be stopped and then thrown back.

On 18th February, on both its corps' fronts, First Canadian Army prepared to mount the assaults the next day which were expected to break the hinges of the German blocking line, Calcar and Goch. In the north German strength increased as two fresh battalions of 6th Parachute Division came in from Holland and took up position between Moyland and Calcar.

Simonds' plan for the attack to start on 19th February was for the 2nd Canadian Division's fresh 4th Brigade to pass through 3rd Canadian Division's tired forward troops and seize objectives beyond the Goch-Calcar road, which had been cut further south by 43rd Wessex on the 16th. At the same time 3rd Division's Canadian Scottish Regiment were ordered to clear the eastern extension of Moyland Woods and to advance and gain more high ground overlooking Calcar.

The 4th Infantry Brigade attacked two battalions up, each supported by a squadron of tanks. The infantry were in Kangaroos and the start line was the road running north-east through Louisendorf. At twelve noon fourteen field regiments, seven medium regiments and two heavy batteries opened fire and the tremendous barrage rolled forward at the pace it was thought the tanks, which were in the lead, could maintain. It had rained most of the night before and once more it was mud that slowed the advance, several Shermans and Kangaroos bogging down in the first few hundred yards.

The battalion on the left, The Royal Hamilton Light Infantry, first ran into mines and then came under fire

A Wasp flamethrower in action

British troops load a rocket launcher

from 88s which forced the troops to dismount well short of their objectives, two groups of farmhouses about a mile east of the Goch-Calcar road, but despite heavy casualties the leading companies got across the road and to within a couple of hundred yards of the farmhouses by 2.30pm.

On the right The Essex Scottish Regiment met with less resistance at the outset and had some of their men in their objectives, the villages of Göttern and Brunshof, by 1.45pm. A half hour later they were strongly counter-attacked. Fighting in and around the buildings went on for over two hours but finally the Essex Scottish had a company firmly established in each village. Prisoners started coming back and by nightfall they numbered a hundred – mostly parachutists.

It looked as though the attack had succeeded and the reserve battalion, The Royal Regiment of Canada, moved up to a line about a mile west of the main road prepared to widen the

captured area the next morning. The Fort Garry tanks were pulled back to rearm and re-fuel. At eight o'clock in the evening both forward regiments reported heavy attacks by Tiger tanks supported by shelling and mortar fire.

Most unfortunately for the Canadians a crack German armoured division, Panzer Lehr, had sent a battle group from Marienbaum, only five miles away, against the RHLI. At the same time Lüttwitz committed tanks and armoured infantry from 116th Panzer Division against the Essex Scottish.

The result was disastrous for the forward Canadian infantry who were quite unequipped to deal with an armoured counter-attack in the dark. The Essex Scottish tactical headquarters and 'C' Company of the Hamiltons were overrun and most of the other companies split up and badly mauled. Survivors sheltered in scattered slit trenches; the panzers searched them out and the shelling and mortaring was non-stop.

About midnight the divisional commander, faced with the possible loss of two regiments, released the Queen's Own Cameron Highlanders of Canada from reserve to the 4th Brigade. This enabled the brigade commander to commit his own reserve, the Royal Regiment of Canada, to battle. A company went forward immediately but returned reporting that the Essex headquarters was 'held by enemy tanks and infantry.'

After the Hamilton's 'C' Company was overrun the battalion commander ordered a counter-attack which restored his defences after two hours' bitter fighting. First light brought a heavy renewal of the German attempts to drive the Canadians off the vital high ground south of Calcar and for an hour or two it was touch and go but a company of the Camerons and a troop of tanks from the Fort Garry Horse arrived just in time to swing the balance. This was followed by a Canadian counter-attack made by the Royal Regiment towards the hard-pressed survivors of the Essex Scottish. Fighting went on all day and the rest of the Camerons and the Fort Garry Horse had to be committed before the German armour was thrown back with the loss of eleven tanks and six *Jagdpanthers*. Greatly weakened, Panzer Lehr was withdrawn from the battle and sent south.

While this desperate struggle had been going on on 4th Brigade's front 7th Brigade on the left had sent their Canadian Scottish to remove the thorn from 2nd Canadian Corps side, the eastern extension of Moyland Woods. German strength was badly underestimated here and Canadian Scottish were under-manned due to heavy casualties in the earlier fighting. The attack was made by a company only sixty-eight strong who advanced against positions held by a newly-arrived parachute regiment. The Canadians were swept by machine-gun fire, mortared and counter-attacked. Only nine men escaped. During the evening the rest of the battalion beat off six attacks by German paratroopers supported by

artillery and one outpost was overrun. The Canadian Scottish lost 140 men during the 18th and 19th of February.

On 21st February the wooded area so stubbornly held by the Germans at last got the full treatment: it was divided into a succession of 300-yard-wide belts each of which was saturated by the divisional artillery and mortars while the anti-tank guns and medium machine guns of the Cameron Highlanders of Ottawa poured in their fire over open sights from the southern edge. This holocaust was followed by two companies from the Royal Winnipeg Rifles accompanied by tanks of the Sherbrooke Fusiliers advancing abreast into the wood. Three Wasp flame-throwers, continually refuelled, moved with each forward company and, the weather having cleared, rocket-firing Typhoons made seventeen separate low level attacks. The paratroopers replied to this tremendous onslaught with concentrated machine-gun fire and deadly 88 air bursts and the Canadian casualties mounted as they moved steadily forward. During the night two sharp German counter-attacks were beaten off and early on the 22nd the Canadians entered the village of Moyland unopposed. The German right wing had pulled back to the line Calcar-Hönnepel. At long last the road to Calcar was open.

But the fighting by II Canadian Corps east of Cleve had been terribly costly: 4th Infantry Brigade's casualties were 400, 7th Infantry Brigade's 485. Calcar still had to be stormed and, after that, the last of the German defence lines before the Rhine, the 'Schlieffen Position' from the Hoch-wald to the Balbergerwald, would have to be broken. For the Canadians bitter, costly fighting lay ahead.

While II Canadian Corps had been struggling to break the German right, XXX Corps had been tackling the immensely strong defence on the left, the bastion of Goch. On the north 43rd Division had followed up their night march by taking and holding seven

Above: 7th Armoured Division troops move into a German village. *Below:* A German border village suffers the damage of war in its streets. *Right:* British Shermans halt on the way up

crossing places over the outer anti-tank ditch and plans now called for 15th Scottish Division's 44th Lowland Brigade, with the help of 79th Division's special equipment, to cross over and breach the second anti-tank ditch, a thousand yards nearer the centre of Goch.

This attack was scheduled for 3.0pm on 18th February but when the brigade commander and the commander of the supporting tank regiment went forward in the morning to assess the situation and got almost as far as the inner ditch without seeing any signs that the Germans were going to defend Goch, they decided to attack immediately by sending a company of infantry and two troops of tanks straight into the city.

The route chosen was that assigned to the 6th King's Own Scottish Borderers but as the leading battalion was the 8th Royal Scots it was they who were sent forward. 'A' Company, with a troop of Grenadier's tanks ahead and another behind, started off just after 11am. All was peaceful and quiet until the point tank arrived just short of the inner ditch when it was hit by a bazooka and blew up. In the resulting confusion a second Churchill got ditched. The leading platoon jumped from their Kangaroos and crossed the ditch on foot in the face of machine-gun fire to establish a valuable bridgehead.

As the attempted *coup de main* had obviously failed the original plan was reverted to except that 'A' Company's forward platoons were left holding the bridgehead on the KOSB route. The rest of the Royal Scots, led by tanks of No. 3 Squadron of the Grenadier Guards, attacked along the right hand route and got across the inner ditch on 'London Bridge', one of the Grenadier's own bridgelaying tanks, and after a sharp action, cleared an area of factories between the railway and the road. Here the infantry and tanks exchanged fire with the German defenders all through the night.

When the KOSB tried to cross the ditch where the Royal Scots platoons were holding the opposite bank they found that one AVRE bridgelayer had jammed its release mechanism, thus blocking its bridge, while a second had slid down the crumbling sides into the ditch. Fascines were sent for to fill in the gap but it was not until 11.30 that night that 'D' Company of the KOSB mounted their Kangaroos and were driven at full speed through the fog and darkness across the ditch. Three carriers were knocked out by bazookas but the men in the others jumped out and stormed the houses from which the fire had been coming and consolidated a tight bridgehead with the forward platoons of 'A' Company of the Royal Scots.

Further to the left 'B' Company of the KOSB had won a grenade-slinging contest with some determined defenders of the Goch-Calcar bridge over the inner ditch and, although the leading platoon lost half its men, had captured the bridge intact and established a small force on the far side.

Thus before dawn on the 19th the 15th Scottish had a battalion well into northern Goch on the right and two small bridgeheads over the inner anti-tank ditch on the left.

The German commander decided that the main assault on Goch was coming from the north from the 15th Scottish and 43rd Wessex Divisions and concentrated most of his forces there, stripping his west flank. The 5th Seaforths of the 51st Highland Division on the other side of the Niers therefore made a crossing of the anti-tank ditch opposite them without difficulty and by midnight an AVRE bridge was in position.

When the 5th Black Watch advanced over this bridge in the early hours of the 19th, catching most of the Germans asleep in their cellars, Colonel Matussek, Goch's Garrison Commander, was captured with all his staff at the breakfast table. But when the following 51st regiments, the 5th/7th Gordon and the 1st Gordon Highlanders, came in the Germans were wide awake and the street fighting became confused and severe. Tanks were bazooka-ed or went up on mines, machine-gun fire swept the streets and the shelling and mortaring was described as the worst since D-Day.

While the 51st were fighting to clear southern Goch the 15th resumed their advance at first light and finished clearing the extensive factory area. They put their third battalion, the 6th Royal Scots Fusiliers, into the town and made visual contact across the Niers with the 5th Black Watch. By nightfall 44th Lowland Brigade had cleared Goch down to Niers. They had taken 600 prisoners (including most of the 190th Fusilier Regiment who had just arrived on bicycles) and cut off a hundred or so other Germans on the right who were scooped up by 53rd Welsh Division.

Fighting for Goch went on for two more days, the southern suburbs proving particularly difficult to clear. Thomashof, a complex of farm buildings about two miles southwest of the centre of Goch, had been made into a strong point and in trying to capture it 'A' Company of the Gordons met disaster losing ten killed, nearly fifty captured and many wounded – there were only two survivors of the attacking force.

As 153rd Brigade had suffered severe casualties the 1st and the 7th Black Watch battalions (from 154th Brigade) came into Goch and continued the cleaning up though not without fairly heavy casualties as the Germans frenziedly sought to avoid losing their anchor position. II Parachute Corps was inserted between XLVII Panzer Corps in the north and LXXXVI Corps in the south and charged with holding Goch, but when its commander, General Meindl, tried to bring his 7th Parachute Regiment down from the Moyland Woods area he found that 43rd Wessex and 15th Scottish had pushed forces eastward to Halvenboom and Bucholt thus cutting his communications with Calcar and Üdem. There was nothing

for it but to fall back to the next Siegfried Line defences.

By the morning of the 22nd February Goch was completely clear and First Canadian Army's line ran for twenty miles between the floods of the Maas and the Rhine. The way lay open for the third phase of Veritable; exploitation across fairly open country to the Xanten-Geldern line. It had once seemed possible that this would start on the third or fourth day. Instead it had taken two weeks and cost 6,000 casualties (of which 80 per cent were British). Furthermore, the Germans were still maintaining a coherent front and it was known that strong fortifications lay ahead.

But the water in front of Ninth US Army was steadily going down and the Germans facing them were now desperately weakened as once again, as in Normandy, they had thrown their armour against the British and Canadians and seen it broken. Grenade was launched at 2.45am on 23rd February, the first possible moment – indeed many thought General Simpson should have waited a day or two more. It succeeded beyond its commander's hopes, for by nightfall the four American assault divisions were across the Roer on a wide front at a cost of only ninety-two dead. It was heartening news for the tired soldiers of II Canadian and British XXX Corps as they made ready to fight again.

The rain had stopped at last and the sun that shone from a new-scrubbed sky had warmth in it for the first time in months. There was the unmistakeable promise of spring in the air, the last spring, we dared to hope, of the war; a spring that might be followed by quiet summer days undisturbed by the blast of guns, shells, bombs or by the screams of the wounded.

We even dared to hope that those terrible sounds would never again be heard in that part of the world which now lay broken and into whose earth so much blood had soaked.

Bibliography

Triumph in the West by Arthur Bryant (Collins, London. Doubleday, New York)
Mailed Fist by John Foley (Panther, London)
Battle for the Rhineland by R W Thompson (Hutchinson, London)
So Few Got Through by Martin Lindsay (Arrow Books, London)
The Defeat of Germany: Victory in the West volume II by L F Ellis and
A E Warhurst (HMSO, London)
The Tanks by Sir Basil Liddell Hart (Cassell, London. Praeger, New York)
A Full Life by Sir Brian Horrocks (Collins, London)
The Siegfried Line Campaign by Charles B MacDonald (Office of the Chief of
Military History, Washington)
The Victory Campaign by C P Stacey (The Queen's Printer, Ottawa)
A Register of Regiments by Arthur Swinson (Archive Press, London)
Hitler's Last Offensive by Peter Elstob (Secker & Warburg, London. Macmillan,
New York)